T0275104

# UNLEARNING SILENCE

life

# UNLEARNING SILENCE

How to Speak Your Mind,
Unleash Talent,
and Live More Fully

ELAINE LIN HERING

PENGUIN LIFE

VIKING
An imprint of Penguin Random House LLC
penguinrandomhouse.com

A Penguin Life Book

LIBRARY OF CONGRESS CATALOGING-IN-PUBLICATION DATA
Names: Hering, Elaine Lin, author.
Title: Unlearning silence : how to speak your mind, unleash talent,
and live more fully / Elaine Lin Hering.
Description: New York : Penguin Life, [2024] | Includes bibliographical references. |
Identifiers: LCCN 2023029717 (print) | LCCN 2023029718 (ebook) |
ISBN 9780593653609 (hardcover) | ISBN 9780593653616 (ebook)
ISBN 9780593832233 (international edition)
Subjects: LCSH: Assertiveness (Psychology) | Self-realization.
Classification: LCC BF575.A85 H46 2024 (print) | LCC BF575.A85 (ebook) |
DDC 158.2—dc23/eng/20231106
LC record available at https://lccn.loc.gov/2023029717
LC ebook record available at https://lccn.loc.gov/2023029718

Printed in the United States of America
1st Printing

Book design by Daniel Lagin

All names and identifying characteristics have been changed
to protect the privacy of the individuals involved.

*To every person who has been silenced,*

*may this book help honor the deepest parts of you.*

# Contents

# Introduction

Everyone knew it was wrong for him to take credit for my work. I was the one who had stayed up late to crunch the numbers. I was the one who had coordinated with the stakeholders. I was the one who had taken and distilled pages of notes into three succinct talking points. Everyone knew it had been me.

Everyone but the executive who mattered.

And yet no one said a word when my colleague took credit.

When the executive praised him for his brilliance.

When my colleague was given the promotion.

I was angry. Angry at him. Angry at others. Angry at myself. Why hadn't I defended myself? Why hadn't I found a way to take credit? It *was* my work. *All* my work.

Yet to say something would seem petty.

To say something would mean not being a team player.

To say something would . . . not really matter.

I hate having to speak up. It's exhausting and, at times, degrading. It means having to parse out why you think what you think and to justify your existence. And if no one else is speaking up or speaking out, it can feel like you're putting yourself in the line of fire alone, without sufficient armor or defenses.

But as the saying goes, if you're not going to fight for yourself, no one else will, right?

From my high school speech coach yelling, "Talk louder!" to the manager at my first job saying, "Tell us what you really think" (but then telling me my thinking was wrong), if I had a dime for every time someone told me to speak up, I'd be retired by now.

Unfortunately, speaking up isn't as easy as simply talking louder. Being free to say what you really think isn't a privilege everyone has.


YOU WOULDN'T HAVE GUESSED IT ABOUT ME—THAT I WOULD HAVE a hard time speaking up.

I hold degrees and teach at some of the best universities in the world. I have the title "Managing Partner" before my name and the initials *JD* for *juris doctor* after my name. I've been in front of audiences of up to three hundred thousand people. I make a living by talking and leading.

Then again, maybe you wouldn't have guessed I'd have a hard time speaking up—you'd have assumed it.

After all, I'm female, Asian, and (relatively) young. It's a well-documented stereotype and statistic that people like me are good entry-level hires but least likely to be promoted to management. People assume that we'll work hard and not cause problems, but they also assume we don't have the vision, self-confidence, skill, and savvy necessary to run the place.

An immigrant from Taiwan to the United States in the 1980s, I was taught to work hard, keep your head down, blend in, and you'll be rewarded for it. It's not all that different from many immigrant stories. The recipe for success was to be *guai*—obedient—and dutifully play the roles I was given.

I am the model minority myth incarnate. Stable two-parent household, straight A student, incredible friends. I went to the University of California, Berkeley for college, because in-state tuition was the practical choice. I studied and have taught at Harvard Law School. I tick all the boxes that are supposed to give you a good life. In some circles, people would say I've made it. So, what is there to complain about?

If success were only about having a seat at the table, then I would be considered successful.

But having a seat at the table doesn't mean that your real voice is actually welcome.

I am consistently called upon to validate decisions from the "minority perspective"—as if I can speak for all women, people of color, and historically oppressed groups. I'm often present so the powers that be can feel good about themselves (or change the statistics in the shareholder report) because the room looks a little more diverse, not necessarily because they want to hear what I have to say.

I am a token, present but silent.

Silence is a survival strategy, to avoid getting on their bad side. Silence means not having to engage in so-called healthy debates that leave me raw and reeling. In some instances, it quite literally means not losing the job that pays my bills.

Silence is what I've learned, internalized, and, at many times in life, been rewarded for.

I've been on team calls where George says Chen should run the numbers because Asians are good at math. I mean, really. Those stereotypes are so old and worn they are like a bad sitcom from the eighties. I let it go, because it's not worth incurring George's wrath.

It's just a joke. It's just George being George.[1] Plus, is what's going on really any of my business? I'm just trying to get work done here. It's easier to stay under the radar.

But if it's not my business, whose business is it?

You may be thinking, *I'd say something. Someone's got to say something, or things will never change. That's just the type of person I am. I do what's right and fight for others!*

But would you?

When you suspect your boss's great idea is going to make your coworker's life horrible, do you say something? When you know the team won't be able to hit the fourth-quarter goals because they were unrealistic, do you say something? When your neighbor's actions are just on the edge of what's ethical, do you say something? When the provost makes an insensitive remark demeaning a student, do you say something? When your friend makes a racist joke at happy hour, do you say something? When your spouse shocks you by mocking a disabled neighbor, do you say something?

These people control your paycheck and promotion. They influence your comfort. They certainly didn't mean it that way, right?

Or did they?

When asked, most managers say they want their people to say something if they see something. Employers want employees to report health and safety violations and bad behavior *before* it becomes an employee relations issue or liability for the company. When asked, most people say they desire trusting relationships with their friends and loved ones. Being seen, known, and heard in those relationships requires us to use our voices.

But how many of us actually do?

There is incentive for each of us to stay silent. For people with traditionally marginalized identities, using our voices can be a new, uncomfortable, and risky venture. How are you supposed to speak up when the world has repeatedly told you that you shouldn't? There is safety and self-preservation in silence. The muzzle might be uncomfortable, but it sure feels more bearable than others' reactions to your voice. Why go through the performative and perfunctory motions of speaking up if you know it's not really welcome, and if in fact, it makes things worse instead of better?

And yet, our individual and collective safety, well-being, and progress require us to use our voices. So where does that leave us?

THIS IS A BOOK ABOUT SILENCE.

How we've learned to be silent, how we've benefited from silence, how we've silenced others—and how we might choose another way. It's about increasing our awareness of what we've learned, and unlearning unconscious patterns so we can make more intentional choices about how we each want to show up. It's about how we can fully unleash talent, speak our minds, and be more complete versions of ourselves—and help each other do the same.

This is a book for people who have been told that using their voice is the leadership skill they need for the next level, who want to get their points of view across in meetings and finally get people to listen.

This is a book for people who have been silenced—who have been told they are not good enough, who have had to carefully calibrate what they can share and who they can be, and who struggle to know what their voice sounds like after so many years of being put down.

This is a book for anyone who wants to be seen, known, heard, and valued, and is coming to the conclusion that the people around you can't support you unless you provide guidance about how they might best do so.

This is also a book for well-intentioned leaders and family members who genuinely want to do better. You believe in honoring the dignity of each human being, but don't yet see how your actions silence the very people you intend to support.

Throughout the book I use *we* to describe us because I am a person who has been silenced. I am also a person who—despite my best intentions—silences people. While the effects of silence are felt most acutely by people with marginalized identities, this book is for all of us—because a healthier way requires each of us.

SILENCE IS BY DEFINITION AN ABSENCE—ABSENCE OF VOICE, ABsence of opinion, absence of life. It starts so subtly that we don't even notice it. We withdraw or withhold our real thoughts from the conversation and replace them with what we imagine others want to hear. But because we hold back, and because we don't create safeenough spaces for people to share, we lose the brilliant idea in the brainstorm or miss the word of caution that would have saved future heart and headache.

Silence is also having to hold your tongue to keep the peace. To choose your words to incur only the amount of backlash you can currently bear. To play the role you're given, rather than the one you want.

Silence is when you're not invited or allowed into the conversation— because there's no room, no welcome, or you're not deemed worthy. Silence is being told to shut up and look pretty, or that the only reason you're still here is because they haven't decided to let you go. It's also when no one has thought to invite you, and you didn't think you could ask.

Silence is when there's not enough air in the room because everyone else's perspectives, personalities, and priorities have already sucked all the energy out. It's overlapping voices that don't include yours, and the exhaustion of trying to get a word in edgewise.

Silence is when you decide your idea isn't worth saying out loud because the voices in your head have already told you it's stupid—just like the kids at school used to say about you. It's choosing not to disclose information and share opinions because it's not worth the energy, effort, or consequences.

Silence is hiding parts of ourselves because they aren't acceptable to others. It's contorting who we are and obscuring who we were meant to be so that other people don't have to face discomfort they don't want. It's denying our own dignity so someone else can have their way.

Silence is wanting to create a space where people feel safe and want to speak up, but you can't get them to do so. It's saying that DEI is part of our DNA but having no idea how to create that genetic makeup. It's wanting to do the right thing but finding that everything you try is wrong.

Silence is the messages we've internalized about what is appropriate, acceptable, or good—messages we've learned over the course of our lifetimes based on what we've seen, heard, and been rewarded for.

Often, silence is the path of least resistance. Too often, it seems the only path. Our habits around silence are so reflexive, we forget we have a choice. When you've learned to live with silence, you forget the possibility of what could be.

THERE IS A PROVERB: *SPEECH IS SILVER, SILENCE IS GOLDEN.*
    Scholars have traced the roots of this proverb back to ninth-century Arabic works, where speech and silence are first connected

to monetary value.[2] And there's no doubt that ancient wisdom and modern practice both tout the benefits of silence. Silence remains a common thread in most religious and spiritual practices. The Hindu practice of *mauna* is a vow to remain silent for a period of time in order to silence the mind. Buddhist monks value silence as a way to practice proper speech and nonviolence. The Bible and Quran both stress the importance of silence and warn about the dangers of the tongue. Silence is what makes mindfulness possible.

Studies show that working in silence requires less cognitive load and results in lower stress levels than working with background noise.[3] Two minutes of silence can lower blood pressure and increase blood circulation in the brain.[4] Duke University regenerative biologist Imke Kirste found that two hours of silence per day prompted cell development in the hippocampus of mice, the brain region related to learning, memory, and emotional regulation.[5] Neurologists look to these findings with optimism for the therapeutic use of silence to heal human brains from damage.

Even the classic Disney animated film *Bambi* touts the virtues of silence: "If you can't say something nice, don't say nothing at all." But who gets to decide what is nice? What if what I say and how I say it doesn't read as nice to you? What then?

If there are so many virtues to silence, why might we need to unlearn it?

MOST ORGANIZATIONS AND SOCIAL GROUPS ARE HOMOGENOUS. THE majority of large companies in the Western world are still predominantly White. Many global companies still have White male leadership. White patriarchy—social organization in which White men hold primary power and privilege—remains rampant. Yes, I did just say White patriarchy—and I'm well aware that it may make me too radical or political in your mind. But homogeneity leads to norms and cultures that don't support all identities. Even when there are a few non-White, nonmale players at the table, their actions (or silence) most likely support the norms of the majority—by design.

This challenge of who determines what's appropriate and acceptable isn't limited to the workplace. Change how you look, what you eat, what you find funny—then maybe the social club or friend group will accept you. We segregate ourselves based on how much money we make, what political and religious views we hold, and who we feel comfortable around. (Economists and sociologists would have me say "sort" ourselves rather than "segregate,"[6] but if the impact is actually segregation, let's call it what it is rather than silence reality.) The communities we live in and the villages we form have the power to support or silence the very parts of ourselves that make us, well, us.

I would know. Since immigrating to the States, I've been on a decades-long journey to fit in. My parents had the privilege of choosing which neighborhood to live in. They chose White suburbia rather than an ethnic enclave and gave me a westernized name because it would give me the best shot at fitting in. In time, being the only non-White kid in school led to being the only non-White partner at a consulting firm.

I used to tell myself that my superpower was being a chameleon, able to blend in with people different from me. It meant I had the skills to work with road maintenance workers in rural Australia and microfinance organizers in Tanzania. It meant I could play the roles needed to connect and have sufficient credibility with corporate executives four decades my senior. It meant I could figure out how to take the feedback that I needed to "be more manlike" when working with the managers of a global insurance company. After all, I knew how to make myself more palatable for other people's consumption.

But along the way, I realized I was losing something in that approach.

Me. My own thoughts. My own feelings. My own ideas. My own sense of being.

I've spent more than a decade facilitating workshops, giving keynotes, and coaching leaders on skills for negotiating, having difficult conversations, increasing influence, and giving and receiving feedback. All skills essential for leading and working in an increasingly automated and disconnected world. While the theories and practices from my colleagues at the Harvard Negotiation Project are sound, I've wondered, Why is it that some people still don't *actually* negotiate or have the difficult conversation? Why, despite begging from leadership and HR, the manager still won't give the feedback and the employee is instead reorg'd or passed on to yet another manager? Why is it that we complain to our friends about the other people in our religious organizations, soccer leagues, and families but don't talk directly with them? Why is it that we need to edit out parts of ourselves to be accepted?

The answer is the pervasive influence of silence.

Silence we've each learned, benefited from, and been rewarded for. We've learned when staying silent benefits us. When silence is considered proper or professional. When it gets us the better outcome—or helps us avoid short-term pain. We're comfortable with silence because it's familiar. It's a coping mechanism and a strategy for maintaining order. Silence leads to a known set of results—primarily, our personal short-term safety and well-being. Biting our tongues keeps the peace at the Thanksgiving table—after all, we won't see them again until next year if we're lucky, right?

These unconscious patterns around silence drive our day-to-day behavior. But without understanding the role silence plays in our lives and how it serves us, we can't make the conscious decision to choose another way.

OUR OWN SILENCE IS ONLY PART OF THE PUZZLE. WHETHER OR NOT we intend to, each of us also silences others.

You may be bristling right now. *I'm not one of those people! I'm kind, inclusive, and welcoming. I watch out for others and lift them up, not put them down.*

I hear you. And if you're human, the reality is that at some point in time, even unintentionally, you've made it harder for someone to speak up. We all have.

I'll be the first to admit it.

When another mom at school asks what my summer plans are for my son, I shrug and say I'm still figuring it out. She quickly responds, "You know that camps are super competitive to get into, right?"

And before I can answer—

"The science programs are the best. They also offer organic lunches."

"Even better if you can get the bilingual program, as it helps with brain development."

"You want him to succeed, don't you?"

I tune her out because I do not need her insistence—however well intended—in my life. The next time I see her, I walk a little slower and linger a little longer on my phone to avoid interacting with her. I "forget" to reply to her texts.

Am I proud that my conflict-avoidant tendencies are on full display? Certainly not.

Is it petty of me? Maybe.

But can I deal with yet another person who wants to dish out unsolicited advice without context? No.

Silence allows me to keep her where I need her—at arm's length.

We've all sent the message that we didn't want to hear what someone had to say. Perhaps because they were wrong. Or we disagreed with them. Or their words stung and we were hurt. Perhaps it was the twelfth question they asked in the last four minutes, and we didn't have it in us to answer yet another "why" question (parents of young children: I'm with you!).

Intentionally or unintentionally, we've all silenced others. But there's no blame here. Instead, I want to help each of us increase our own self-awareness so we can show up more like the versions of ourselves we want to be and create spaces where belonging, dignity, and justice are realities.

UNLEARNING SILENCE REQUIRES AWARENESS AND ACTION, SO THIS book is structured in two parts.

The first part focuses on raising our individual and collective awareness of the silence we swim in and contribute to each day. Chapters 1 to 5 set a baseline understanding of the silence we've learned, and how we silence ourselves and silence other people. The second part of the book offers practical strategies for using your voice and building families, teams, and communities that support rather than silence. In essence, chapters 6 to 10 will give you practical advice on what to do differently.

For those of you who—like me—are action-oriented, please don't skip over the first five chapters in order to get right into action! Behavioral change without cognitive and emotional understanding of what is at stake and why the change matters can be empty—and is far less likely to stick. Creating space for your and others' voices isn't just about saying the right words. Unlearning our current habits around silence requires a fundamental understanding of why silence is problematic. Unlearning silence also requires each of us to cultivate a willingness to incur the personal and social discomfort necessary to develop new reflexes. In chapters 1 through 5, I'll help us build that awareness with as much clarity and compassion as I can muster.

## A THOUGHT

I've had the unique honor of facilitating the conversations people don't normally have. Whether it's the unfiltered diagnostic call where direct reports say what they really think about their managers, or the leadership team meetings where decisions are made, or people not realizing I'm bilingual and talking as if I didn't know the language, I've gotten to hear what people really think and feel.

Throughout the book, I use a combination of case studies, research, and personal examples. The case studies are based on experiences people have shared, dynamics I've observed, and conversations I've been part of. I also include everyday examples between friends, family, coworkers, and community members that might seem innocuous to illuminate how wide-reaching and invasive silence is in our lives.

From gender, race, and ethnicity, to age, education, birth order, and beyond, we each hold so many identities. Where a specific identity is a primary factor in what a case study intends to illustrate, I name the identity. That means choosing to identify and capitalize each individual's racial identity, including White. Where an identity may not be a primary factor for the specific example, I omit the detail to try to highlight the universality of our human experiences. Even if you don't hold the same identities as the individuals in the case studies, I invite you to consider how the dynamic impacts you and the people around you.

If we want to be heard, and if we want to create spaces in which other people can be heard, we have to understand how power, identity, privilege, and learned patterns lead us to silence. We need to support voice by managing the role silence plays. We need to understand and actively choose our own relationship with silence. We need to unlearn the ways we silence ourselves and silence others. We need to unlearn silence.

# Part I

---

# AWARENESS

# 1

# The Silence We Learned

don't want to go to Aunt Becca's house. It smells there!" yelled five-year-old Charlie.

As quickly as she could, Charlie's mom shushed him. "C'mon, Charlie. Be kind."

"But it's true," he pressed.

Charlie's mom thought for a minute.

It was true. Not even the industrial-strength air fresheners or the fancy new air neutralizer she'd bought from the shopping network and gifted Becca could mask the cat odor. If she was honest with herself, she didn't love going to her sister's house either.

"Still, Charlie," she said sternly, "she's family. We have to go."

"I still don't wanna."

"Doesn't matter. We're going."

Charlie pouted but went along.

Like Charlie, we all start out life with opinions and preferences—of where we want to go, what we want to do, or what environments we prefer. But over time, in the name of propriety and respect, many of us learn not only to stay silent about those thoughts, but that those thoughts don't matter. Our families and friends reinforce those norms and calcify them in the spirit of what is good, proper, or normal. We form reflexive habits for when we silence ourselves and silence others based on individual, structural, social, and intrapersonal experiences.

In this chapter, I'll talk more about how silence shows up in each of the above areas, so that you can better understand how it appears and shapes your day-to-day life. My hope is to bring what is often unconscious into the conscious, so we can make more informed choices about whether those messages and habits serve us today.

## WHAT IS VOICE?

Voice is the opposite of silence.

But voice is more than saying something in a conversation. Voice is the expression of our beliefs, values, opinions, perspectives, and uniqueness. Voice is using our thoughts, ideas, and actions to shape the world around us, expressing what we believe matters through our words and actions. Voice is the freedom to believe, speak, and live, showing up as we each intend, rather than how others intend. Voice means playing a part in making decisions about your own life and the lives around you. At the end of the day, our voices are what we dedicate time, energy, and effort to.

## How We Learn Silence

Each of us has a unique relationship with silence, one based on the messages we've received over the years about when, where, how, and with whom it is okay to share parts of ourselves. Without understanding the influence of the silence we've learned, it has power over us—an invisible force that impacts our lives, but that we can't control or shape.

But when we begin to understand the contours of our existing relationship with silence, we can also begin to question which of those learnings still serve us, which of those learnings we want to experiment with, and which we might leave behind. Unlearning silence doesn't mean that we cast aside everything we've learned or that we always say everything. Rather, it means having a conscious awareness of our learned defaults around silence so we can evaluate whether those are defaults we want to keep or evolve.

I know of no other way to unlearn silence than to interrogate and reckon with it.

Moving forward, we'll explore the many ways we learn silence. As you read the next sections, I encourage you to reflect on the following questions: What messages have you internalized about who gets to speak and be heard, and whose voice matters? What reflexive habits have you developed around using your own voice or supporting others' voices? How well do those habits serve who you are today and who you want to become?

## On an individual level

Simone always felt torn about Sunday dinners with her extended Italian-Irish-American family. On one hand, she loved getting to play hide-and-go-seek with her cousins. She loved the bustle of a house filled with people and the mix of savory and sweet smells coming from the kitchen. She couldn't wait for her grandmother's luscious Sunday gravy—a secret recipe that Nonna had promised to share with her one day.

At the same time, the visit always seemed fraught. No one knew quite when Grandpa would blow up. Or when he did, what the cause would be. One minute, he was warm and cuddly, inviting the kids to sit on his lap while he pretended to be Santa Claus. The next, he would turn into a grouch that no one could please. The joke was that you had to feed Grandpa enough snacks so he wouldn't get hangry.

When Simone asked her father why Grandpa acted that way, he replied, "Grandpa's complicated."

One Sunday as they sat down to dinner, Simone was sharing about her new bike. Her dad had saved up to get her exactly the bike she wanted—a two-wheeler with red streamers, kickstand, and shiny bell. The bike was the most beautiful thing she had ever seen, and she had taken good care to polish the bike after riding it to keep it in perfect condition.

Overhearing the conversation, her grandpa chided her, "Don't you go showing off, Simone."

Simone wanted to say that she wasn't showing off. That she was just sharing her excitement. That she was grateful for the gift. And that it wasn't fair that Grandpa was picking on her. But she knew better than to say anything back. She had watched others in the family try to explain themselves over the years. Doing so never ended well.

Grandpa turned his attention to Simone's father. "What are you doing spoiling that girl? You're going to make her weak."

Simone watched as her father avoided Grandpa's glare and nodded, looking for a way out of the conversation.

Grandpa went on, "Do you hear me, boy? Don't go raising soft kids. We don't need any more brats in this family."

The words stung everyone around the table. Wearily, Simone's father suggested they give thanks for the food.

None of us came out of the womb with the reflexes around silence we have today. But like Simone, we start learning pretty quickly.

As babies, we cried. We cried when we needed something or were upset. We cried to communicate. It's well-known that if no one responds, babies eventually stop crying because they learn the futility of asking for help.[1] Most of us were shushed (understandably!), soothed, and eventually told that big boys and girls don't cry. We were taught to suppress—or regulate—our needs and emotions.

This learning continued as we grew older and began to register the responses we got from people around us, particularly our families of origin. Were you rewarded for being well-behaved and not expressing your needs and desires? Think about what is okay and not okay to talk about in your family of origin. The weather, what you ate for lunch, and what you know they want to hear? Typically safe. What you saw on the news, read in a book, or heard on the radio? Mostly benign. Politics, religion, weight, money, dating, feelings, and what you really think? Often questionable if you want to remain unscathed.

Generational differences also shape the silence we learned. A 1951 *Time* magazine article was the first to dub people born from the late 1920s to 1945 the Silent Generation.[2] Living through the Great Depression and the tumult of World War II meant that people around the world learned to work hard and keep quiet. Strict discipline and being "seen but not heard" characterized childhood.[3] In the United States, the House Un-American Activities Committee and McCarthyism's investigation of citizens suspected of political disloyalty during those years also had a silencing effect.[4] From the government to Hollywood, people lost reputations and jobs if suspected of having communist ties. So they kept their thoughts to themselves and spoke only when spoken to, lest they be accused of something they didn't do. Even working quietly and not doing anything that would call attention didn't always protect people from being accused of disloyalty.

We learned what we can talk about, with whom, by the reactions other people had—by how much we were shushed and how much wrath we incurred. We also learned whether to stay silent based on how those around us chose to respond. We learned when and where to stay silent based on which of our behaviors were rewarded and how the behaviors of those around us were received too.

## On a structural level

What Simone learned about staying silent at Sunday dinner served her well in school. Her report cards came home noting that she followed instructions the first time they were given and that she listened attentively and respectfully, making her a great student.

The comment from Simone's teacher was revealing—Simone wasn't a great student because she was smart, hardworking, or always had the correct answer. According to her teacher, Simone was a great student because she was obedient and didn't cause trouble in the classroom. She could memorize times tables and repeat them back. She could parrot back the answers she knew the teacher was looking for. Her reward for the memorization and parroting was her teacher's affection and approval. Her compliance—or silence—was her greatest asset. She met the structural expectation, again, that children should keep quiet and be well-behaved.

In contrast, her classmate Henry was curious. He had a lot of questions. When his teacher asked him to name a country in South

America, he responded, "Bolivia! Did you know that Bolivia has the largest salt deposit in the world? And during the wet season the water turns the salt flat into a large mirror?"

"That's enough, Henry," his teacher responded. "We only need the name of the country."

Frustrated, Henry bit his lip. He had been so excited to share about the salt flats, as his mother's family was originally from the flats. It was one of the times that he actually knew the answer to his teacher's question. Tears welled up in his eyes, and his chin wobbled.

"Haha! Henry's crying again," taunted one of the kids in the class.

"Kids, let him be," said their teacher.

Kids ask roughly 125 questions per day. Adults ask about 6 questions per day. Somewhere between childhood and adulthood, we silence our curiosity.[5] Like Henry, we learn compliance to the rules and norms that govern the spaces we occupy. We stop asking why because it annoys the authority figures in our lives, gets us in trouble, and isn't necessary for the standardized test. We learn not to think for ourselves, but to produce the output that people want from us.

School systems are set up to favor a narrow set of skills and forms of expression that play to the strengths of a few. Music and art are considered extracurriculars, the first to be cut when the budget is tight. We are subtly encouraged to stifle our uniqueness in order to fit the mold of what the classroom rewards. We see that people who don't fit the dominant expectations are policed, labeled "at risk," pushed to the margins, and ranked as "less than."[6] We learn that only a certain type of voice matters, so we begin to silence our creativity.

## IN SUPPORT OF TEACHERS

Many teachers do an amazing job of cultivating curious, brave spaces that support individual uniqueness. Most of the people I know, myself included, can recall a teacher who influenced our lives and helped us become who we are. That's the gift of good teaching.

That said, to understand the complexity of structural silence, we must first acknowledge the other structural challenges schools face. Underpaid and overextended teachers work to ensure that students can score well on standardized tests that determine how much funding the school will receive. Everything from class size to lack of funding to political pressure requires teachers to work pure magic. The observation of what traditional education supports and silences is not a knock against teachers. Teachers themselves have also learned silence. The observation is an urge to examine how we might evolve our practices to better support voice—for students, for teachers, and for the generations to come. It's an invitation for teachers and students alike to create brave spaces—classrooms where people don't have to leave part of themselves at the door to feel a sense of belonging, where it's safe to try new things, and where we normalize discussing and addressing things that make us uncomfortable.[7]

Students in traditional classrooms learn by reading and listening, rather than debate or discussion. But studies show that if rote memorization and regurgitation alone are rewarded, we fail to develop critical thinking skills.[8] People who express differences of opinion are considered combative, problematic, or challenging. This approach to learning reinforces the norm that one should only speak when spoken to, particularly when confronted with an authority figure, and fails to cultivate creativity, collaboration, communication, and self-directed learning—the skills deemed critical for living and working in the twenty-first century.[9]

Learning is inherently vulnerable. We can't learn when we feel foolish asking questions or that our opinion and experiences aren't of value. Like Henry, being told that your enthusiasm and family background aren't welcome suggests that *you* aren't welcome.

Additionally, students often aren't offered the whole story. Like most of my peers, the history books I read in elementary school celebrated Christopher Columbus's discovery of America. He was a hero to be admired. My eight-year-old mind didn't know that the rape, exploitation, and murder of Indigenous and Native peoples were conveniently left out. Like me, students (and often parents) don't realize that the silencing of voices is happening, as we internalize the erasure embedded in curriculum.

People and organizations who develop curriculum and content have the power to paint the version of history they want us to see. Representation of different identities in education materials informs students about what society expects of them and others based on social identity.[10] Not talking about privilege, race, class, religion, gender, sexual identity, and ability doesn't make those parts of our lives disappear. Instead, being silent about those parts of life and history sends the message that we don't recognize those parts. They don't matter, and the people who are impacted by them don't matter either.

And it's not just in school. We take these lessons with us throughout life.

Years later, rule-following Simone faced a rude awakening. Her manager had said she should always go to him with problems before they got worse. But when she expressed her concern about unrealistic deadlines, he replied, "Just make it work."

It can be hard to voice concerns at your job. Most leaders say they want to build a speak-up culture: "Tell me about it before it becomes a crisis." But often, leaders send subtle messages about what they *truly* want to hear. Whether it's okay to raise concerns about pay equity, sexual harassment, misogyny, or not being able to meet the quarterly targets all depends on manager reactions. When managers respond to employee perspectives with resistance or denial, employees are most likely to believe speaking up is not worth the risk or effort.[11] These norms lead to organizational silence—an academic term for not saying or doing much about issues—because people believe speaking up is not worth the effort and that voicing one's opinions is dangerous.[12]

What we implicitly learn and teach each other is that we have to keep our thoughts to ourselves in order to stay employed or in good relationship with one another. We learn that silence is the answer to controversy and conflict.

## On a social level

Jess met up with a friend of a friend. It was supposed to be a professional networking opportunity. When she went to pay for parking, she realized the machine only took cash. She didn't have any on her, so the friend of a friend suggested she come to his hotel room where he could lend her some cash. When they arrived there, he forced himself on her. She screamed no, but he wouldn't let her out of his grip, and wouldn't let her out of the room until she promised not to tell anyone what had happened.

For years, Jess didn't tell anyone. She had watched women in the news get ripped apart if they came forward to share that they'd been violated. The victims were called sluts, told that they shouldn't have worn those clothes or put themselves in the situation. They were accused of coming forward in order to extract a financial payout from their attackers.

In that kind of climate, Jess wondered if she said something, who would believe her? And what difference would it make? She felt ashamed that she had "let it happen," beating herself up and replaying the events. What was she supposed to have done? How else was she supposed to break into the inner circle in the industry? No one in her family or among her friends understood that world. If the real deals happened on the golf courses or between fraternity brothers, what hope was there that she could make it? Men got to grab drinks with other men; why couldn't she? She hadn't sent any signals that she was open to anything. They had talked about zoning and licensing laws, for goodness' sake. Nothing else.

We learn silence based on how people in similar situations have been treated. The majority of people who experience sexual violence do not report the violence, in part because of how people who have come forth have been ostracized, blamed, and dragged through the mud.[13] Social, emotional, and sometimes legal barriers prevent people like Jess from talking about their experiences, while they are left to suffer in silence and go through life as if it's business as usual.

I recently learned the phrase *Snitches get stitches*. Meaning, if you report someone to an authority, you'll be the target of retaliatory violence.[14] The exact origins are contested, but the phrase refers to a code of silence where involving police could inflict harm on the community.[15] I came across the phrase because my son said a kid at preschool broke a toy. When the kid's father overheard my kid sharing, he quipped, "Watch out. Snitches get stitches." A far cry from rightful distrust of a discriminatory justice system.

At first, I thought "snitches" was a Dr. Seuss reference. But then I realized, this saying—dropped so lightly in casual conversation—is yet another way we learn silence. If you report someone or share something—even in preschool—you're branded the tattletale. And in some contexts, "tattling" literally gets you killed. But how are we supposed to talk about things and troubleshoot issues and adopt different behaviors if we've learned that the costs of speaking up are ones we can't or don't want to bear?

Our collective responses to incidents determine whether stigma and social cost will prevent people from reporting and seeking help, and whether we believe authorities will be helpful. We learn that silence, however painful, at least seems less painful than having others doubt, question, or tell us that what we lived through couldn't really have happened.

We also learn who gets to speak and who is supposed to stay silent from how the media portrays people who look like us. A study of 1,300 popular films between the years 2007 and 2019 by the USC Annenberg School for Communication and Journalism revealed that only 30 percent of the speaking characters were female. That means that viewers see 2.2 males speaking for every 1 female speaking.[16] Of the Black, Latinx, Asian, or LGBT characters in the films, very few of them had speaking roles. Only 4 out of 26,618 characters were transgender, and had a grand total of 2 minutes of screen time combined. According to this slice of media, it is normal for men to speak. Women, non-White people, LGBTQ+ people, and people with disabilities are supposed to stay silent, if they are part of the fabric at all. This portrayal of society enters our subconscious data set of who is worthy of being on the big screen, who gets to be a hero, who gets to be a leader, and who gets to be heard.

## On an intrapersonal level

Growing up, the norms in my Asian American and Christian church communities were clear:

*Don't talk back.* This was the ultimate sign of disrespect. Talking back meant to challenge, to express a different view, to ask a genuine or leading question. When told to do something, I was supposed to comply.

*Respect your elders.* Respect meant not pushing back, not going against their wishes, not countering what they said—at least not directly or publicly. After all, they had lived longer, so they knew better.

*Don't air your dirty laundry.* Family business is family business. I would never have told anyone if my parents were fighting or if we were worried about money. All that was to stay within the family. And we certainly wouldn't talk about emotions.

Having internalized these rules, my defaults were to shut down and stay silent.

If interpersonal communication is the interaction between two people, intrapersonal communication refers to the messages we send to ourselves. Being a rule follower, I took these rules to heart and started telling myself the same things. I learned to silence myself.

I'm trying to unlearn this silence. And now, as a parent, I'm working to figure out which rules I want to pass on and which generational patterns I want to break.

Do I want my child to talk back? Not really. When it's two hours after bedtime and said child is only halfway down the list of reasons why he can't sleep, do I want him to shut it? Yes. But do I also want him to have his own opinion, learn that there is power in using his voice, and not have to unlearn the things I learned? Absolutely.

Do I want him to respect his elders? Yes, but not at the expense of losing his own opinion or ability to develop his own thought process.

Do I want him to share what's going on in our family? I want him to be able to seek social support, benefit from the connection of community, and make wise choices with agency about what he wants to share or keep to himself.

I'm convinced that adulthood is an ongoing process of figuring out what we learned in our childhood and years after, and then figuring out what we want to keep or supplement. I'm constantly taking the responsibility to understand why the things I've learned can be problematic. Awareness of these learned defaults means that I (and you) can make conscious—and potentially different—choices going forward.

IN THIS CHAPTER, WE'VE EXPLORED THE WAYS WE'VE LEARNED silence—through our individual experiences, through social structures like school and work, and through our own thoughts and internalized beliefs. What does your own relationship with silence look like? Where and when do you consciously deem it appropriate to use your voice? Which parts of you do you feel the need to withhold or edit out?

I encourage you to interrogate the silence you've learned, because my learned silence isn't just about me, and yours is not just about you. Our learned silence is about how we show up in relationships, on teams, and in community, and the way those defaults shape the world.

# REFLECTION QUESTIONS

---

What have you learned about silence . . .

   from your family of origin?

   from your school days?

   from your work experiences?

   from the cultures you are part of?

# 2

# The Problem with Silence

Vince was a managing director at his company. He had taken the role because the company was on the leading edge of the industry. The opportunity to innovate in a market that had largely been run the same way for decades was appealing to him.

Yet in meetings, when other people pushed for creative ways to structure deals, Vince began to notice that the structures didn't seem right. But he was a mathematician and economist, not an accounting expert. He was worried about raising the issue because he had seen others who had questioned the company labeled as "not smart enough to get it."

When he finally did flag his concerns, he was shot down. When he spoke up on a management call, he was cut off. He stopped getting invited to meetings. One day, he got the call that his group was going to be transferred to another division because they were inhibiting rather than supporting processes.

The company Vince was working at was Enron—the energy company that was once the seventh-largest company in the United States. As head of Risk and Research at Enron, Vince Kaminski's job was to make sure the company was not taking excessive risk. But when he refused to sign off on a certain deal structure, he received complaints about his work. Other leaders at Enron silenced Vince by cutting him off in conversation, transferring his group to limit the impact of their work, and refusing to heed his warnings.[1]

The end result was the largest corporate scandal in modern history, with losses of more than $60 billion in shareholder investment and five thousand employees losing their jobs without severance or medical insurance.[2]

ECONOMIST ALBERT HIRSCHMAN NOTED IN HIS 1970 TREATISE THAT when things aren't working, people's options are to exit a system, try to use their voice to change the system, or stay loyal to the system.[3] When voice isn't welcome, exit becomes appealing. After that, the only people left are the loyal ones—the ones who play by the rules that leadership has crafted. Having only loyal employees creates an echo chamber that might feel empowering in the moment but leaves no opportunity for course correction.

You might be thinking, yes, but that was Enron. It wasn't silence that led to Enron's downfall. It was misappropriation. It was fraud. It was a lack of checks and balances. It was ego. There was no internal audit function.

You would be correct. But silencing others is what enables wrongdoing, greed, and arrogance to go unchecked. In fact, silence is a common factor in all corporate scandals of the twentieth century. In each instance, there were people who tried to speak up but were ignored, dismissed, disparaged—silenced—by others. Being repeatedly shot down and forced to absorb the costs of speaking up dulls our instincts and ability to see differently, much less be able to ar-

ticulate differences of perspective. That's not to mention the structural silence already in place by the absence of certain voices and
functions within a system.

Silencing people creates groupthink, where the desire for consensus and harmony overrides common sense, expressions of alternatives, critiques of position, or unpopular opinions.[4] If you choose
to stay in a system, you say what is expected of you rather than what
you really think, because that is what the system rewards. What is
rewarded becomes the rule.

And people tend to obey rules, especially if the rules come from
an authority figure.[5] In a series of studies now well-known as the
Milgram experiments, participants were asked to administer elec-
tric shocks of increasing voltage on others. Some participants expressed concerns as the voltage increased and they heard screams
from the recipients, but continued administering shocks when they
were told by the researcher they wouldn't be personally held responsible for the outcome and that their help was required for the
experiment. Sixty-five percent of participants were willing to go up
to the maximum 450 volts, even when worried they had killed the
subjects.

Not only does silence mean that there's little opportunity for
course correction, that the people with opposing views leave, and
that you're left in an echo chamber of "yes men."

Silence also leads to negative health effects.

Having to hide part of one's identity and watch what you say
keeps our nervous systems chronically on high alert. The levels of
resulting stress manifest in skin rashes, digestive challenges, heart
issues, migraines, and adrenal and chronic fatigue.[6] Silence is a
common response to trauma,[7] and forced silence can be considered

secondary trauma.[8] In contrast, being truly heard and seen by people is the most powerful protection against being overwhelmed by stress and trauma,[9] which cannot happen if we remain silent or are silenced.

In this chapter, I'll further explore the problems with silence, explaining how being silenced leads to self-doubt, contributes to erasure, and exacerbates suffering. And I will show how silencing people—intentional or not—shapes our perception of reality and perpetuates the problem by creating even more silence in the world.

## A CONFESSION

I hesitate to write this chapter because in the wrong hands it could be used as a blueprint for inflicting harm on people by purposefully silencing them. I also realize that my hesitance to articulate what is problematic about silence comes from my own scars from having been silenced. In fact, the very dynamics I write about are the ones I navigate as I write. Is there something worth saying here? What if people exploit the flaws in my argument? How will I respond to the inevitable backlash? The challenge of being silenced is that you edit yourself before you even begin to speak.

But for me, analyzing what's problematic about silence is worth the education for those who haven't experienced the relentless, unyielding impacts of silence and the validation of those who have.

I hope you feel the same.

## Silence Leads to Self-Doubt

Patricia is the only woman on the otherwise all-male executive team at a biotechnology company. Despite holding an MD-PhD in biomedical engineering and having an impressive résumé as an industry veteran, she's perpetually told by her fellow executives that she is too emotional, too scattered, too empathetic. Over time, the narrative that she's not "leadership material" has calcified. Anytime she raises a work-culture issue in executive meetings, the reaction from her colleagues is "There goes Patricia again." But then in her annual review, she's told she doesn't engage enough in executive conversation.

Having to constantly prove herself makes Patricia doubt what she brings to the table. The truth is, though, that *she's* the company's best asset. *She* is the one who brings the inspired ideas the company relies on, and *she* is the executive key to employee trust and retention. But you would never know it by attending the executive meetings. Over time, she's chosen silence because it is what incurs the least criticism from others.

At home, the situation is no better. From organizing the family's calendars to arranging for someone to finally fix the leaky sink, Patricia is the one who makes the family run—despite the fact that both she and her husband have demanding full-time careers. Even as she acknowledges her privilege in being able to afford help, she's still the one who gets every call—from school, doctor, dog walker, nanny, housekeeper, friends, and family. And inevitably, she's the one who is blamed when there isn't food on the table or the kids misbehave.

Every time Patricia has tried to negotiate for a more equal split of household labor with her husband, he has pushed back, saying, "Do you not see how tired *I* am?" Somehow the conversation turns so that any conflict is Patricia's fault. Apparently, she's the one who is ungrateful, has unrealistic expectations, and doesn't contribute enough. She leaves these conversations feeling dismissed and disrespected, especially because she has already silenced so many of her own hopes, dreams, and needs to make the family work. Over time, she stops even trying to have the conversation. Her frustration turns to anger, and anger to resentment.

On the worst days, being bombarded by messages at work that her ideas aren't enough and at home that her efforts aren't enough, Patricia begins to doubt herself at every turn. *Maybe I'm overreacting. Maybe I am oversensitive. Maybe I misinterpreted it. Maybe I just don't understand how things work here. Maybe it's me.* She begins to think that she's not good enough.

Much like Patricia, when people fail to recognize our contributions and dismiss our thoughts, we can start to wonder if we are the problem. We doubt our instincts. We begin to assume that other people's gut instincts, analytical ability, and decision making are more valid than our own. We forget that our values and spidey sense are hardwired to scan for threats, and that our perceptions are valid. Over time, our intuition and gut sense are so muted we fail to hear them at all. Instead of looking at what outside of us might be wrong, we start to think we ourselves are wrong.

Consistently being diminished and dismissed means that we forget that we are worthy of respect, dignity, belonging, and love. That our worth isn't determined by what we can do or achieve, but that by nature of being human, we are worthy of respect, dignity, belonging, love—and so much more.

So it may go against everything your colleagues, family, and the system are saying to you in words and action—but let me say it:

You matter.

Your thoughts, concerns, questions, fears, and preferences matter.

## Silence Infringes Dignity

Sociological studies have demonstrated in study after study that people who hold more dominant identities have more power in a system. In much of the world, that means White, wealthy, able-bodied, cisgender, male. Those who have more dominant identities inherently have an advantage, get to make the rules, and receive the benefit of the doubt. Their voices are accepted by default because they are the norm. Those who have more subordinated identities start with a disadvantage, have to follow the dominant rules, and, by nature of not having the dominant identity, are seen as deficient, or as the other.[10] Those with subordinated identities are told to acculturate to the dominant norms. Having your voice—rather than a stripped-down, culturally appropriate version of your voice—heard is inherently an uphill battle.

Take Hadiyah, for example.

The daughter of one of the first Black female cardiothoracic surgeons in the United States, Hadiyah was always taught to celebrate her Black heritage. Throughout college, her sorority sisters kept her grounded. When Hadiyah started her first job, as a marketing coordinator at an advertising agency, her manager recommended she straighten her naturally curly hair to appear more "professional." Not wanting to be well-known to HR from day one, Hadiyah traded her hoop earrings for subdued studs and beloved high-tops for "practical" flats. When she brought leftover spiced lamb and rice for lunch, someone commented loudly about the smell and spritzed air freshener around the office. Hadiyah began to feel like the only way she would ever make it was to be someone other than herself. Clearly, her real self wasn't welcome.

For employees like Hadiyah, it can often seem like the only way to keep their hard-won job is to blend in. And even then, a place isn't guaranteed.

Being asked to tamp down or edit the parts of yourself that are different from others is a form of silence. The "constructive feedback" Hadiyah receives is about making her look and act a certain way based on the expectations of those in power. Often done under the guise of cultural fit or doing what the elusive customer would prefer, the suggestion that Hadiyah change herself silences her uniqueness. Being told that parts of who you are need to be edited out conveys the message that you are here for your utility, rather than your humanity.

## CONFORMITY IS ABOUT CONTROL

Some of you might be thinking—isn't asking people to change their behavior just part of grooming someone new to an industry? There is a certain way that things are done here, and what you're doing is not it. You're not it. If you want to be here, you'll need to fit in.

Fundamentally, silence can be an aesthetic—a preference for how things are done and a means to maintain the way that things are done.[11] One person's joy is another person's noise. When certain people or groups of people get to decide what is acceptable and allowable, silence becomes about control.

I'm a realist. And part of being a realist is to acknowledge that each organization, team, family, and system has a set of preexisting norms. They are often invisible, but no less influential. So while it's perhaps a pipe dream to overturn norms as well-worn as the marble steps inside the leaning tower of Pisa, awareness of what we're asking of one another and why allows us to examine why these norms exist in the first place. Are the norms we're supporting the ones we intend? Do they support the culture and world we're trying to build—on this team, in this system, in this family? How might we be using silence to erase people?

## Silence Erases Our Sense of Selfhood

Motherhood has been one of the most humbling experiences in my life. I have never been so tired or incoherent—or so covered in someone else's vomit. Everything becomes about the child. *Are they fed? Are they breathing? Are they okay? What do they need?*

Juggling another human being, in addition to all the others you previously supported, is not easy work—it's no wonder so many women report losing a sense of self in the early days of raising a child.[12] The hungry baby who needs a midnight feed has no regard for your body clock. My toddler calls out at 11:00 p.m., 3:37 a.m., and 5:45 a.m. His long wails of "Moooommm" are both sweet and maddening. It has been five years since I've slept through the night, and my child is only four. In the seemingly impossible choice between being present for him and my own needs, I've been conditioned to believe that the right choice is of course to take care of him. After all, a good mother is selfless and self-sacrificial.

And it's not just mothers. Girls are socialized from a young age to believe that caring for others is women's work.[13] Women are expected to sacrifice their time, ambition, and sense of selves for others.[14] As sociologist Jessica Calarco notes, "Other countries have social safety nets. The U.S. has women."[15] When families, schools (hello, PTA!), communities, and societies rely on women's selflessness to run, we are expected to silence our own needs for the greater good.

When we spend so much time solving for and supporting other people, our own needs and preferences get muddled. There's been much said about the "second shift" of both invisible and all-too-real labor that women do at home after their day jobs. But what rarely gets talked about is how we silence our own needs. When you learn to put everyone before you—as most women around the world do— you barely have time for a shower, much less the solitude and time needed for reflection and to care for yourself. And in this frame, no one else has been taught or conditioned to care about our needs. So we go without our needs being met.

When the world hasn't been about you, it's easy to forget that you have needs and a voice. Being silenced—verbally or structurally through social conditioning—makes us forget that taking care of ourselves is an option.

## Silence Dulls Our Ability to Think for Ourselves

Thiago was the eldest grandson in a close-knit Brazilian family. There was no doubt that his grandmother was in charge—they called her Lala to her face, reserving "the witch" for when she wasn't within earshot. As a child, Thiago watched as his father followed Lala's every order. Even when his father had a different opinion, he ceded to Lala's directions. *Trust those who have lived,* she'd say. *We know better*. He saw the toll it took on his father and vowed not to do the same. Lala wasn't reasonable, but that didn't matter. The people who had questioned her became family folklore—the people who shall remain unnamed.

When she passed, everyone breathed a sigh of relief. But her ways lived on. When Thiago was unable to hit his quota for new customer registrations at work, his manager told him to round up the numbers. Doing so didn't seem ethical to Thiago, but he figured that his manager had been in the industry for longer and knew what he was doing. Without realizing it, Thiago was living by Lala's rules—trust those who have lived longer. He rounded up the numbers. The team celebrated hitting their targets. "Way to be a team player," said his manager.

Every once in a while, Thiago would think, *This doesn't seem right*. But his manager had told him not to worry, and as he looked around, his peers were all doing the same thing. The higher-ups were happy. They were lauded as the fastest-growing branch of the company. Thiago was promoted.

It wasn't until years later that the auditors would discover the errors and fine the company, and Thiago would wonder why he had listened to that manager. Why hadn't he questioned the practice more in the moment when, in retrospect, things were so clearly right and wrong?

Each of us spends time solving for the concerns and priorities of those around us, particularly when we are more junior in organizations or feel the weight of pleasing other people. We channel what we've seen leadership do because those are the behaviors that get rewarded. We act as deputies of the organizations we work for and the people we love. We're not alone: of the more than fifty-eight thousand employees who worked at Facebook at the time, Frances

Haugen was the only one who chose to go public with concerns about the company allowing hate and illegal activity to go unchecked.[16]

Even when we experience internal struggle about what those around us are doing, there are often incentives to squash the nagging voices. From reporting radioactive material[17] to price-fixing to safety violations to discrimination, throughout history the cost of reporting has included retaliation, harassment, blacklisting, losing your job, and receiving death threats. It's safer not to stick your neck out. So we silence ourselves and keep on going.

But the net effect of biting our tongue or choosing compliance is not only all the instances where we didn't speak up, but also that our own instincts dull over time. After years of solving for everyone else, and often being rewarded for doing so, we can forget that we have values, thought processes, and opinions of our own. We lose the power of our own voices because we forget we even have them.

The question that's missing is, what do *I* think? Not what does the organization think, or what does the leader think, or what would they do? But what do I think? What will I do?

## Silence Exacerbates Existing Suffering

Andrew was a Hispanic educator, active in his rural college community and beloved by his students. Each semester, evaluations raved, "Andrew is the best. He brought engineering concepts to life in a practical and accessible way." "The course was life-changing." "I never knew that I could master technical concepts. Andrew made learning fun and helped me believe in myself."

Despite the positive reviews and stable social connection, Andrew struggled with constant anxiety. It felt like his heart was going to thump out of his body. It was hard to take a breath. In classrooms, he clenched his hands to try to hide the trembling. High functioning and charismatic in public, no one knew of the panic attacks that brought Andrew to his knees in private.

*What will they think of me if they know? They are talking about budget cuts already. I can't give them reason to put me on the chopping block. I can't afford to lose my job. I don't want to be a burden. I don't want them to think I can't cut it.* Brought up in a home where sharing what you were struggling with was a sign of weakness, Andrew kept his worries to himself.

In one of the *Mario Kart* video games, players can buy a badge called "Double Pain." If Mario has the badge, any damage dealt to him is doubled.[18] I'm struck by how often we, like Andrew, wear Double Pain badges by staying silent.

Whether it's a disappointing grade on an exam, an unwelcome medical diagnosis, or an interruption to our carefully planned programming, life deals us blows. Those blows themselves hurt enough. But to feel like we have to carry on as if everything is fine and there is no one we can tell—that we are sworn to secrecy to carry the weight in isolation—is another level of pain.

Social isolation is comparable to smoking and obesity in terms of shortening one's life span.[19] Loneliness contributes to lower levels of health, risk of cardiovascular disease, elevated blood pressure, and functional decline.[20] Our social ties—being known by others and not going it alone—provide a buffer against stress and anxiety.[21] It's not to say that talking about things with others doesn't come with its own costs, but carrying things alone doesn't help.

Many of us buy into the myth that we have to go it alone. We've learned, often with good reason, not to trust those around us with our pain. But the repression of emotions also suppresses our body's immune system, making us more vulnerable to illnesses ranging from colds to cancer.[22] Studies of patients with cancer show that those who mask their experiences and feelings are more likely to die despite treatment than patients who express their experiences and feelings.[23] The amount of relief from pain and discomfort reported by patients with chronic illness has been found to be commensurate with how much they can deeply and authentically express their emotions.[24]

There's certainly a cultural component to all of this. Individuals from cultures that value the collective over the individual are more likely to suppress their emotions than those from cultures that value the individual over the collective.[25] For example, Asian Americans have historically rated open displays of emotion as less appropriate than European Americans[26] and are more reluctant than European Americans to seek social support because we worry about burdening others.[27] It's not the emotions themselves that cause vulnerability to sickness, but the protracted reliance on emotional regulation that allows disease to thrive.[28]

Luckily, Andrew broke his silence. After months of suffering alone, he picked up his phone and started a text to a friend. "Hi—I'm having a hard time. I'm not sure what's going on. I don't want you to fix me, but I at least wanted someone to know." He erased and retyped it multiple times. And finally hit send. The reply came almost immediately. "Thanks for letting me know. I don't have answers, but I want to support you. I'm here." Double pain reduced.

There are certainly times when it makes sense to keep things to yourself, and in the next chapter we'll explore those benefits of silence. While there might not be quick fixes to the underlying pain or injury, connectivity can be a balm for the double pain of isolation and what is sometimes self-imposed silence.

Who might you be able to share with? Who would you trust? When you reach out, tell them what role you want them to play or not play, or what you know or don't know. The goal isn't for either person to have the answer, but to take the sting out of having to suffer in silence.

## Silence Shapes Our Perception of Reality

Jerome was the founder of a local fitness group. Having moved to town not knowing anyone else, he was looking to connect with people. A lifelong fitness buff, Jerome had always appreciated the camaraderie and accountability of working out together. Surprised that there weren't any organized groups, Jerome decided to start one. He posted on local message boards and organized weekly meetups with different workouts. Starting something from scratch and engaging strangers took a lot of vulnerability, but as people showed up, he started to see the payoff.

Jerome had always prided himself on being positive. He liked to cheer people on. When things got tough, he'd push into another gear. He was the one who could get you through the pain and strain of the fifth set of squats and the last mile of the run. When people griped, he told them it was all part of getting stronger. The more people complained, the more he pointed to what was great.

Over time, fewer people started showing up. At first Jerome thought it was just the changing of the seasons. But as the months passed and Jerome found himself standing alone at their meeting point in the park, his motivation to organize waned. If people didn't care enough to be consistent, why should he?

When Jerome ran into people around town who used to be part of the group, they were polite but quick to get out of the conversation. Jerome started to wonder what was going on. It had just been fitness, for goodness' sake.

One day when Jerome happened to be at the same coffee shop as a former group member, he asked. "Hey, what happened? Why did you stop coming?"

"You really want to know?" she inquired.

Puzzled, Jerome said, "Yes, of course."

"You're just too damn positive. Everything had to be great, or good, or fantastic. The group felt toxic."

"Why didn't anyone say anything?" replied Jerome, trying to curb his frustration.

"It didn't seem like you wanted to know."

Jerome was gobsmacked. He'd put all this time and energy into creating a community, and people didn't have enough respect to say something to his face? When was the last time being too positive was a problem? If the way he was running things was so offensive, why hadn't someone said something?

Not all silence is caused by shutting people down or cutting them off. What Jerome didn't realize is that whenever a single perspective dominates, important information is left out—even when that perspective is intended to be encouraging. Jerome had created an environment in which people didn't feel comfortable telling him how things were really going. His enthusiasm, however well intended, made people uncomfortable *and* silenced group members from telling him what needed to change. Instead of speaking up, Jerome's community just stopped showing up.

This is not an unusual dynamic. Getting people to share what they really think is a careful dance—a tango between a willingness to ask for feedback, receptivity to what people have to say, the history of learned silence, and a level of investment in the relationship. We cannot learn if people aren't willing to share, and people usually aren't willing to share if they feel silenced by us or have been silenced by others. Like Jerome, without the information and the ability to hear that information, we're left in our own skewed sense of reality.

We live in a world in which we can curate the information we consume and the people we interact with. What happened with Jerome's group happens online every day. Being able to ghost opinions we don't agree with and people we don't like is alluring because it's easier to avoid engaging with things that challenge us. And yet the echo-chamber effect of silencing other voices has left us more divided and less able to engage across differences.[29] When we don't see or engage with ideas (or people) that don't fit neatly into our world view, we also lose our ability to engage thoughtfully with people and perspectives different from our own. It is easy to demonize people when we aren't face-to-face, by simply swiping on our phones.

This curation matters because what we see and hear profoundly shapes our understanding of the world. What is silenced by society also tends to be absent from the media we consume. Consider that 90 percent of the two hundred top-grossing films released between 2017 and 2019 in the United States and UK Commonwealth countries did not have any Muslim characters in them. Of all the speaking roles in those movies, only 1.6 percent of the roles were held by Muslim characters. The majority of the Muslim characters were set in the past, either spoke no English or spoke English with a foreign accent, and were either the perpetrators or victims of violence.[30]

What critics have termed the "epidemic of invisibility" is a silencing of complex, multifaceted human beings. This representation shapes and supports the narrative that Muslims are terrorists, people of the past, perpetually foreign, and that women, if present at all, are defined by their male counterparts. This form of silence perpetuates stereotypes, shapes public perception of people groups, and fuels real-world consequences. What is seen and celebrated is normal. What is silenced—not seen and not celebrated—becomes abnormal.

Our understanding of what is normal based on the media we see and the inputs we have in our lives also shapes our understanding of what is acceptable. What voices might we have silenced that are skewing our view of the world? What questions are we not asking that shape our reality? Asking questions and being able to hear different perspectives is not just about people being treated with dignity, it's a way to safeguard against being caught off guard. We are weaker when we're missing information. Without input, we cannot learn.

## Silence Breeds More Silence

Marianna bit her tongue as Chad, the CEO, tore her presentation apart—and she was only on slide two.

"This is irrelevant."

"This is grounded in speculation, not in fact."

"How can we trust you to advise the company if you don't even get the company?"

The rest of the meeting was a blur as Marianna worked to maintain composure.

After the meeting, colleagues privately reached out to see how she was doing.

"They didn't set you up for success."

"It was completely uncalled-for."

"I can't believe how rude he was."

With each call, what struck Marianna most was that none of these now-concerned colleagues had said anything as they sat *in* the meeting.

Silence breeds silence.

Not saying anything publicly sends the message that we only talk about things privately, if at all. Our choices in the moment either challenge or reinforce the preexisting cultural norms. We justify our silence in the moment (sometimes rightly so) as necessary for our own self-preservation or to avoid being on the receiving end of the vitriol. But we often forget the second-degree impact: the less people speak up, the less likely anyone is to speak up. More specifically, the less people *in power* speak up, the less anyone speaks up. It's not to say that some things shouldn't be handled privately, but that the conversations that are visible are the ones that become the culture.

When Marianna later asked her colleague Jing, "Where were you during the meeting?" Jing didn't have a good reply. As much as he didn't want Marianna to be on the receiving end of Chad's ire, he certainly didn't want to be on the receiving end either. His seat at the table as someone who wasn't yet vested at the company was precarious, and Marianna's cause wasn't the primary one he was trying to get across the line this quarter. He needed to be on Chad's good side to get approval for the budget. Plus, everyone knew that Chad had bad days. Chad was as volatile as he was passionate. And it was his passion and commitment that was going to drive the company to a successful IPO, or so went the story everyone told.

While Jing's calculation is understandable, his silence, like the silence of folks within Enron and Facebook, signaled consent to Chad's behavior. Our silence leaves people who have been attacked vulnerable and isolated. Our silence tells people the behavior is acceptable and that we'll allow the behavior to continue.

Teacher and blogger Boaz Munro notes that silence is part of an ancient, toxic pattern that enables genocide. Political tensions arise and one group is attacked. People turn their backs and disaster ensues.[31] In each individual moment, silence might not feel like we're turning our backs, or that we're perpetuating racism, but the cumulative effect is deadly.

Our silence desensitizes us. We brush offenses off because if we considered every infraction, we wouldn't be able to function. *It's just men being men. It's just the end of the fiscal year; they're really crunched. It's not worth the fight.* We justify behavior and choices. But these justifications are a coping mechanism. When we have less power in the equation, our emotions cooperate with our brains to moderate the insult and anger we feel. In proper measure, this collaboration reduces potentially damaging friction. If overutilized, we develop unsubstantiated trust in authority figures, which means we stay silent and don't question their behavior. That silence enables abuse, condones violence, and can perpetuate oppression.[32]

Rarely can one person alone define a culture. Yet everyone's behaviors either disrupt or perpetuate a culture of silence.

AS WE'VE SEEN, THERE ARE SOME REAL PROBLEMS WITH SILENCE and being silenced. Silence chips away at our sense of self and erases what is unique and valuable about each of us. It makes our existing suffering worse—and God knows there's enough suffering in this world already. It limits our ability to thrive and create a world in which the people around us can also thrive.

So if you're looking for quick fixes, I'm sorry to disappoint. If it took us decades to learn the silence we know, it's not going away overnight. But what I can offer you is this: if we can see the contours of silence more clearly, we can realize when it's happening, why it's happening, and begin to choose different ways forward.

# REFLECTION QUESTIONS

In what ways has silence shaped
how you use your voice?

How do you see silence impacting
the people around you?

What parts of yourself might you
currently be silencing?

# 3

# When Silence Makes Sense

As the only non-White attorney at her law firm, Grace was exhausted. Not physically exhausted, but emotionally exhausted.

She didn't want to have to explain—again—that the model minority myth was in fact a social construct designed to drive a wedge between Black and Asian folks and reinforce White power. She didn't want to have to explain the weight she felt from her parents working 24/7 for below minimum wage so she could go to college and "have a better future." She didn't want to have to share why it was offensive for her colleagues to "accidentally" call her Jessica—the name of the only other Asian person in the office. She wanted to shout: *Jess is Korean and from California. My name is Grace, I'm Chinese and from New York. We are two different people from two different states that are three thousand miles from each other!*

Grace's coworkers and manager were always telling her that she was too quiet and that she needed to speak up more. Her friends told her that if she wanted things to change, she would have to be the change she wanted to see. But when she tried to share her opinion, it was as if others didn't hear her. Or if they did, it would turn into feedback about *her*. Having to clarify *again* that she wasn't Jessica seemed futile. After all, she'd always been mixed up with the only other Asian or Asian-looking kid in the class. "No worries, I respond to being called Jennifer too," she'd say with a light chuckle, remembering the other Asian girl in her grade school. In doing so, she was affable and easygoing. Her coworkers invited her along to happy hours. She felt like she finally fit in. Or she thought she did.

Two years into her time at the company, HR required all employees to take an unconscious bias training that talked about microaggressions. Early in the training, someone pointed out that the microaggressions weren't actually so micro. In fact, each and every one was a violation of dignity. When Grace started to pay attention, she noticed the violations were everywhere. That meeting where the client assumed she was the assistant rather than the lawyer? The compliment saying that she was really articulate? Being paraded out every time the team needed to demonstrate diversity, but otherwise being sidelined?

At some level, Grace pined for the days where she didn't see the violations, because ignorance was in fact bliss. Now that she saw them, she couldn't unsee them. She had to do something about them. She wanted to be part of the solution rather than perpetuate the problem. So Grace began to call out the violations, offering feedback to the individual, using the construct she had learned in a leadership course:

"When you said this . . . the impact on me was . . ."

Sometimes people would be receptive. Sometimes people would be defensive. But for Grace, it was always exhausting. The violations were so frequent that calling them out, explaining why they were offensive and why people should care, dealing with the backlash, and carrying the emotional labor was turning into a full-time job. And she already had a full-time job—as a lawyer.

WE ALL LIVE THE SAME TENSION GRACE EXPERIENCED.
If we don't call things out, it's unlikely people will know that something happened or that their behavior had a negative impact. When we do call it out (or call people in), it still takes mental, emotional, and relational energy that is finite for each of us. And if we speak up, there's no guarantee that it will be received well; it might even make things worse. Which is why only a third of employees have conversations with their managers about leaving before quitting, even if 52 percent of employees believe their manager could have done something to prevent them from leaving.[1] And it's part of why only half of people report always speaking their minds at work.[2] If you take the time and energy to raise something, and you don't know if it will make a positive difference, why *would* you do it?

Unlearning silence isn't about always speaking up—the world is too noisy and too complex for that. Unlearning silence is about being aware of when you are silent, and whether that silence is one that you've chosen or whether it is chosen for you.

## A NOTE ON GUILT

If you've been feeling guilty because you've been thinking "I should have said something . . . ," "I can't believe I didn't do more . . . ," "If I'd only said something, it would have been different . . . ," please let go of the guilt. It's possible you could have said something and it would have made a difference, and depending on how you're situated, that may or may not be your work to do.

Professor and psychiatrist Pooja Lakshmin notes that guilt comes from the contradictory expectations that ask us to serve others without taking up any space of our own. Chronic guilt is yet another way we silence our own thoughts and feelings.[3]

Every individual shapes the world, but no one is solely responsible for it. So please, free yourself from the burden of self-flagellation. I don't want the guilt or the "should haves" to be another thing that weighs on you. "Should have" serves no one unless you turn it into action, and which action you choose is going to depend on a set of factors only you can evaluate.

## Three Questions We Wrestle With

We intuitively wrestle with three questions when deciding whether voice or silence makes more sense: 1) What are the costs of choosing voice? 2) What are the benefits of staying silent? 3) Given the costs and benefits of voice and silence, what makes sense for me? In this chapter, I'll explore each question to validate the—perhaps many—times we've chosen silence. If you've never struggled with silence and find yourself judging those who do, I hope this chapter sheds some light on the complexity of factors that incline people around you to silence, and that it helps you evaluate when you choose silence. (And in chapter 9 you'll find concrete ways that you can help change the calculus of whether it makes sense for people around you to choose voice instead of silence.)

# What Are the Costs of Choosing Voice?

Every decision between voice and silence includes conscious or unconscious calculations as to whether the costs of using your voice are ones you can—or want—to incur. In addition to the obvious costs of having to deal with someone's reaction, being told you're wrong, or experiencing retaliation, the costs of engaging the unknown, navigating someone else's rules, and losing control also influence our decisions to stay silent. Any of these costs alone can be enough to incline us toward silence.

## Engaging the unknown

Jim was a charmer. As a White man who had been the star of every lacrosse team he'd ever been a part of, he thrived in the spotlight. Put him in front of a crowd, and he could raise money for causes like nobody else. The problem was, Jim was also incredibly disorganized, never replied to emails, and espoused what many believed to be conspiracy theories. Melissa had tried raising the issues with him, but to no avail. "C'mon, Melissa, it's all just part of my genius," Jim would say. Jim's inability to work with others was a pain. But the amount of money Jim was able to raise for Melissa's sports therapy nonprofit made the trouble of working with him worth it. That is, until one of the event coordinators told Melissa that Jim had disparaged attendees at the last event. Worried about her organization's reputation, Melissa vowed never to collaborate with Jim again. She wasn't going to take on the liabilities that came with working with him.

But as their spring fundraising drive approached, the board members asked, "What about Jim?" Melissa thought, *Well, maybe.* No one could tell the story of their work as powerfully as Jim. Maybe he'd be more responsive this year. Maybe he wouldn't mouth off behind the scenes. *Or even if he did, at least we know how he is,* thought Melissa.

"Better the devil you know than the devil you don't" is an oft-repeated proverb. It captures the Latin phrase *Nota res mala, optima,* which translates to "An evil thing known is best." We tell ourselves it might not be ideal, but at least it's easier to know what's coming.

Change is hard. Figuring out a new situation, a new relationship, and the contours of a new context is real work. Uncertainty intensifies how threatening a situation feels to us because it inhibits our ability to avoid or mitigate the threat.[4] So much so that researchers have wondered whether the unknown is actually the fundamental fear.[5] Like Melissa, if we at least know what we're dealing with, our brains can be prepared. Trying to get Jim to change had been an unfruitful waste of time. Trying to find someone who was as good at fundraising had also proved an unfruitful waste of time. It made more sense for Melissa to stay silent about Jim's liabilities and work with the devil she knew.

There are times when taking on the unknown feels too costly. As much as we might dislike the status quo, we at least know how it works. Speaking up and trying something new introduces uncertainty. Silence at least is familiar.

## Navigating someone else's rules

One executive recently said to me, "I don't mind if people speak up, so long as they do it respectfully, professionally, and at the right time and place."

Her comments are the heart of the issue. People in power determine the rules and norms for using our voices. *When* we're supposed to talk. *If* we're supposed to talk. *How* we're supposed to talk. I'm allowed to speak up, but only on *your* terms. Having to calculate whether what I say fits into your mental model of how I'm supposed to show up is exhausting. And what is "professional" is often code for workplace practices that privilege the values of White and Western employees.[6] What is respectful behavior will differ across cultures. The rules of engagement are often unspoken and subject to change. So silence offers a seemingly safe retreat when you can't or don't want to conform to someone else's preferences—or when they keep changing the rules on you.

Many of us face what social psychologist Adam Galinsky calls the low power double bind—if you don't speak up, you go unnoticed; if you speak up, you get rejected, all because you're outside the range of acceptable behavior.[7] But who gets to decide what is acceptable behavior, much less, an acceptable range of behavior? Or whether you can expand the range of what is acceptable?

The answer? Typically the people who currently hold power.

Remember, those who hold dominant identities tend to have the most power. Lest you think this is just another tirade against able-bodied White cisgender men, I'll note that unlearning anything simply requires acknowledging reality.

In this case, the reality is that women make up 51 percent of the U.S. population, but only 8.1 percent of CEOs of Fortune 500 companies.[8] And as of the writing of this book, only two—or .04 percent—of those CEOs are women of color. Only 40 percent of women—less than half—are satisfied with decision-making processes at their companies.[9] And even if data shows that diverse teams, particularly teams with diverse leadership, outperform nondiverse organizations financially, progress is slow.[10] Why? Because it is hard to give up power. It is hard to share power. And power is often invisible to those who have it.[11]

Code-switching—adjusting your language, style, speech, behavior, and appearance to optimize the comfort of others to try to get fair treatment[12]—is exhausting. Trying to avoid or defy stereotypes takes energy and can hinder performance.[13] Trying to pretend you conform when you don't is draining.[14] It's all invisible work that we're doing—all. the. time. This labor lands with the people carrying the most subordinated identities—and it is work those with dominant identities don't even realize is taking place. After all, things have always been that way.

To be clear, as a consultant who works across industries, organizations, and borders, it is on me to adapt my style. Being able to lower people's defenses, help people feel connected, and hear the things they need to hear is what makes me good at my job. And as a human who strives to be kind and considerate to others, it is on me to "read the room" and acknowledge the data people are giving me and take that into consideration.

What is not on me is the constant, unrelenting need to quickly calculate what I'm going to say, whether I'm going to say it, how much blowback there's going to be, whether I have energy or capacity to take it, what impact it's going to have on my career, or how it's going to change the relationship in my own home or on my team *because* of the identities I hold. It is on everyone to create that space so that the costs aren't disproportionately borne by the people who have to do the most work.

When I visit my closest friends, there is an ease in the interaction. There's no need to explain why you would take your shoes off when you enter the home. There's no question that you would clean out the leftover food scraps from the kitchen drain. There's no awkward moment as to whether we're going to pray before a meal. There's no wrinkling of noses at the fermented black bean sauce—only acknowledgment that it is delicious. Perhaps this is why people tend to seek out those who are similar to themselves.[15] There is an ease that comes with shared norms and understanding. You don't have to explain yourself as much. You don't have to negotiate the rules as you butt up against someone else's expectations of how you should be showing up. You don't have to plead for people to see and value your humanity. You don't have to incur the costs of figuring out the unwritten rules and deciding whether to challenge, modulate, or conform to them.

## Losing control

*I wish you had never been born. Keeping you was the worst decision I ever made.*

Regret set in before Sara finished saying the words. She hadn't meant to say it. She was just so frustrated. So angry. So worn. It wasn't fair that she was left to raise this child on her own. That the father just disappeared one day and moved on with his life as if nothing had happened, as if life hadn't been brought into the world. She'd tried so hard to make things okay—working multiple jobs, extra shifts, maxing out credit cards. She asked favors from people she barely knew so that someone would keep an eye on Theo while she tried to make life work.

Even without looking into Theo's eight-year-old eyes, she knew things would never be the same after those words. The damage was done. The blank look in his eyes would be an image seared in her heart. Maybe he was too young to really know what that meant. Maybe he wouldn't remember. Maybe getting the toy he wanted would help, she thought. Nothing did.

It was not how she meant for things to go down. Having grown up in and out of foster care herself, Sara had been determined that things would be better for any kids she ever had. And things were supposed to get better. Money was supposed to start coming in. But the checks never arrived. At times she really did regret keeping her son, but she also knew it was one of those things she probably shouldn't have said—at least not to him.

That moment shaped how Theo saw the world; how he saw himself. After that, he withdrew. *If my own parents don't want me, who would?* It played out in his relationships and affected whether he could be in them. It would be decades before the pain of rejection and alienation would start to heal.

That moment haunted Sara too. Since the different ways that she tried to make it better didn't help, she stopped trying. At least Theo was grown and out the door. But later, as she reflected on that moment, she realized that at the time, what she really meant was, *I don't know if I can do this. I don't know if I can raise you alone.*

Emotions cloud our judgment. Stress compounds it. It is good to release and process those thoughts. Just not always with the person they are about. Because once the words are out there, you can't take them back.

Sharing our thoughts and moving through the world in the way most authentic to each of us means that we open ourselves up to inputs from other people. We can't control the impact that we will have on the people around us and how people will react, but we can control what we put out there. Choosing voice means that you could lose control.

## What Are the Benefits of Staying Silent?

The second question we focus on when choosing between voice or silence is about the benefits of silence. In reality and perception, silence is often what allows us to survive, care for, and protect our-selves. In this regard, silence becomes a strategic choice that allows us to maintain baseline sanity, the ability to perform day-to-day life tasks, and a semblance of dignity.

## Silence allows for survival

Gloria lived in the shadows. She remembered the bright orange flowers, green mountains, and sweet scents of her family home in El Salvador. She also remembered the terror of the guerrillas pounding on the door and the constant fear she and her family would be killed. After the last time men stormed their home and demanded her father give himself up, her family decided it was time. They walked for weeks. They would not stop until they reached the United States. Her throat stung because of how parched she was. Drinking water from the trough intended for horses in the middle of a dusty storm was something she would never forget.

Gloria and her family made it. On the other side of the border, they were safe. They could have a better life. Her mother cleaned houses for a living, paid in cash. Her brother kept the yards of the fancy houses fancy. They made money to send back to relatives. They didn't have a car or a computer, but they had one another. It was far better than being killed.

But there was a new threat: the threat of being discovered.

Gloria and her family had crossed the border without documentation. If they were reported, they would be detained and separated from one another. Or worse, sent back to a country where it was likely that Gloria wouldn't live to her eighteenth birthday. Kids at school would talk about the illegals—how they were horrible, violent, and stealing from this country. Gloria kept her mouth shut. Her parents had made it very clear they should never mention how they had gotten here. They should never make trouble and never answer the door if someone knocked. It was the only way they would be able to survive. For Gloria and her family, staying alive and staying together required silence about their status and history.

Whatever our stance on the complex topic of immigration, we each make choices that keep our loved ones, careers, hopes, and dreams alive. What we keep to ourselves or share with others allows us to—literally or figuratively—live another day. Silence allows others to believe what they want about us in circumstances where disclosure drives a wedge. It allows us to trade in the gray.

There are places and times when our well-being, livelihood, and futures are at risk. Voice—saying something, being something different from the status quo—is inherently threatening because it is a change-oriented behavior. It represents attempts to claim status, and for that claiming to work, it must also be accepted by others. But we can only get that status if it is aligned with others' expectations of what to expect from us.[16] It's no surprise that many large corporations actively try to prevent workers from unionizing and not every country gives its citizens the right to vote. When I ask people the primary reasons they don't speak up, the responses are typically some combination of not wanting to damage a relationship, lose a job, risk an existing dynamic, or have to deal with another person's reaction. Silence affords us the benefit of avoiding all those things.

Very few people would blame us for running for our lives if the building we were in was on fire. In fact, most people would support our choice to run. After all, we're under attack. What we fail to realize is that as far as our brains are concerned, psychological safety—defined as the absence of interpersonal fear[17]—matters as much as physical safety. In nonthreatening situations, the prefrontal cortex is in charge, allowing us to think rationally and logically. When our brains detect a threat, the amygdala—or emotional part of the brain—takes over while our prefrontal cortex goes offline.[18] Whether the threat is a physical fire or an email, our brains act similarly, ready to address the perceived threat through fight, flight, freeze, or fawn.[19] In fact, an attack on one's psychological safety can have a deeper and longer-lasting impact on the brain than a physical punch to the face.[20]

## Silence protects my energy

It has been more than a decade since the conversation, but I still remember the feeling clearly. I was excited to catch up with my friend. On our walk, we talked about the things that two single people in their twenties might talk about—work, friends, who we were dating, or had just gotten out of dating. When I shared that my love interest at the time couldn't yet commit to being my plus-one at an upcoming wedding, my friend replied, "Sheesh, why can't they get it together? What do you see in them anyways?!"

The minute she said that, I regretted having told her anything. She attacks my significant other; I have to defend my life choices. I wanted to snap back, "You've misunderstood, I'm supposed to be the one that gets to vent, not you." Instead of our friendship being a safe space for me to vent about what seemed like an entirely normal set of "getting to know someone" issues, I felt like I had to defend myself—my choice to spend time with them, invest in them, explore with them. My decision making, character, and soundness of mind seemed like they were on the line.

Was I overreacting to my friend's comments? Perhaps. But it takes energy to deal with people's reactions—to decide whether to engage with, let in, or negotiate yourself out of the impact of their feedback. It takes energy we often do not have, or would not choose to put toward that cause.

Disclosing information opens you up to commentary about it. Instead, it can feel easier not to tell people anything about your life. Silence in the form of selective disclosure is a way to avoid judgment or criticism.

While it comes at the cost of intimacy—knowing and being known deeply by someone—not all relationships have to be intimate. Some just have to be functional. Having to deal with judgments and reactions can deplete the limited storehouse of energy we have for navigating day-to-day life.

## Silence is self-care

Having been in the industry for more than a decade, I shouldn't have been surprised by the request. After years of not acknowledging race, an older White male collaborator asked: "Can you tell me more about what it's like to be a person of color? I'm leading a session next week for people of color and need to know how to reach them."

Hearing the ask, I had nothing nice to say. To lump everyone in the same group, assume that one person could speak on behalf of the global majority, or that one conversation would make this person even close to being equipped not to continue doing damage was pure hubris. Trying to extract my life experience for their benefit when they were ready reeked of entitlement. I wanted to shout: *My stories and life are not here for your consumption! There's something called Google. Look it up.*

It didn't help that a few days earlier, I'd received a text from a friend who confessed, "I know so little about race, it's really quite embarrassing."

And a message from a White family member saying, "I read this article and realized that minorities in our country have a lot in common with each other. It would be great to discuss with you."

Hard pass. Delete. Ignore.

What I wanted to say in each situation but did not have the energy to say was—I'm glad that you're developing an increased awareness of the dynamics that people navigate every day. I do not want a front-row seat to your racial awakening. Being in relationship with you means that I will have to witness your process, but I'll take the balcony seats—back row, please.

It's taken me a long time to get to this clarity. I spent years as one of the few non-White people in the very White field of corporate education. When events needed cross-cultural fluency, I was a go-to. When we needed to demonstrate that the ivory tower wasn't just for White people, my name came up. When clients wanted more diversity in their otherwise all-White male speaker lineup, I was an easy solution. Except, of course, when I wasn't "diverse" enough because I wasn't Black.

I bought into the color-blind ideology for years. I had grown up believing in the ideal of America as a meritocratic melting pot. Whether at work or at school, I was used to being the only minority. In a twisted way, it felt nice to be needed. By sticking it out, I felt like I had survived. I had figured out how to contort myself into being okay with being useful. Ignoring race was how I could stay in the field—not explicitly, of course. But implicitly. Because seeing how inequity is baked into a system makes it untenable to stay day to day, when you have the option to leave. Once you see inequity and ignorance, they grate at your soul.

When a team I'm part of was redoing its website, someone noted that we looked like a really White team—because, at the time, the majority of the team and all of leadership, other than yours truly, was White. The suggestion? Make my picture on the landing page larger. As if the size of a photo would solve what was problematic in both perception and reality.

Until then, I didn't realize how weary I was from trying to stay in White spaces. I always thought I was good at modulating. Prided myself on it, in fact. I could imitate the speech patterns, sense of humor, and stance of the successful White people around me. The schools I attended and the socioeconomic class and leadership level I entered gave me plenty of privilege. But all that doesn't protect you from death by a thousand paper cuts.

Being "the only" in any context is a special kind of low-grade pain. You contort yourself to fit in, because fitting in seems like a ticket to acceptance. You're celebrated for your difference when convenient and dismissed when your utility is over. You lose yourself because it's hard to sustain uniqueness when conformity is what's rewarded. You question your value. You question yourself. You feel like you have to represent your entire race, gender, or identity because people draw conclusions about those populations based on their interactions with you.

And sometimes, sharing who you are is not worth the pain that comes with doing so. If others are going to challenge something so fundamental, so core to who we are, and rip us apart, why would we share? If our explanations and attempts to educate are dismissed on whatever grounds they choose, why try to engage at all?

We are not intellectual exercises.

The challenges I have faced—and so many face in far greater intensity—are not interesting topics to spar about at your leisure. They are day-to-day lived reality. To stay sane, to stay functional, to have something left of ourselves to care for, we need at times to stay silent—to draw boundaries that protect us from you chipping away at what's left of us.

Activist Audre Lorde says your silence will not protect you. While that's true and a fundamental tenet of this book, sometimes it's enough to preserve what's left of you to get you to the next day.

Workplace trauma is real.

Racial trauma is real.

Homophobia is real.

Sexism is real.

Xenophobia is real.

Ableism is real.

Classism is real.

All of these influences chip away at who we are. The cognitive and emotional labor required to code- and context-switch is work we unconsciously do and that is invisible to those whose actions require that we do it. Compound these influences through the lens of intersectionality, and it quickly becomes clear why self-preservation is necessary.

Self-preservation is the fundamental tendency humans and animals have to protect themselves from harm or death and maximize chances of survival.[21] It's the instinct to flee from dangerous situations or predators. For jackrabbits, that means running from the fox. For humans, it can mean saying no, getting restraining orders, or not replying to the email. But our instincts can be dulled. Our bodies find ways to cope. Our alarm systems recalibrate. Our ability to feel and imagine decreases.[22] We walk around as shells of the people we could be. In a capitalistic world that will consume and use as much of us as we're willing to give, preservation is the baseline.

While self-preservation is about existence—being able to keep something whole—real self-care is about nourishment—being able to provide the conditions for growth that prevent us from getting to depletion. The Black Panther Party in the United States promoted the message of self-care to Black people to prioritize looking after their own health and well-being, as it was necessary to remain resilient in the face of relentless systemic and medical racism.[23] Which means self-care cannot only be about bubble baths, massages, and "treating yourself." It is allowing yourself to be silent when you need to create the conditions for your own nourishment. Preservation is about surviving; care is about thriving. We all deserve both.

Women of color make up only 39 percent of women in the United States but represent 89 percent of new women-owned businesses. Hostile work environments and perpetual pay inequity (Black women continue to be paid 37 percent less than White men for the same work) drive Black women to leave corporate America.[24] Because if you can't get a seat at the table or the seat at the table doesn't really mean anything, and you want to preserve your dignity, self-worth, and sanity, you have to build your own table.

It's not worth turning yourself inside out day after day to maybe get the scraps of what others might be willing to throw you. It's not worth having to contort your speech, your values, your style, your thoughts in order to stay. It's not worth losing yourself to make the profit-and-loss statements look better at the end of the quarter. So we preserve ourselves by not giving of ourselves. We draw lines of what topics are off-limits. What relationships we engage in. The parts of our lives that we're not going to let you in or be privy to. It is a way to stay sufficiently whole and craft a life that's still worth living.

The constant barrage of underinformed comments against the backdrop of systems that prioritize the needs and wants of certain populations over others means that those with subordinated identities need to draw boundaries that support our own existence and tend to our own well-being. Sometimes that means not replying to the text message. Sometimes that means exercising emotional restraint.[25] Sometimes it means keeping a distance.

Sometimes that means staying silent.

## THIS IS NOT A PASS

As humans, we often misinterpret, take out of context, and strip the nuance away from things that are hard to hear. So let me be as clear as I can—knowing that silence can make sense does not give us a pass. Silence can make sense *and* we need to interrogate when and where we choose silence.

We are not all equally situated. For people with historically oppressed and underestimated identities, silence is a survival strategy. For us, I advocate making choices that make sense for your survival, sanity, and self-care. Navigating the ongoing destructive realities, trying to heal, and trying to change the world at the same time is too much. Prioritize what you need in each moment and season.

That said, I ask those with privilege—and I count myself among them—to interrogate what we are really choosing when we choose to stay silent. Are we choosing our own comfort and status over someone else's dignity? And is that the choice we want to make?

Be honest: Do you have privilege from being male or able-bodied or light-skinned (this includes but isn't limited to

White!)? Do you have privilege from holding a senior position at work or having more than six months' worth of living expenses saved or not having people depend on you for caregiving? This is not a knock on your identity. Instead, having privilege(s) means the risks for choosing voice aren't as high. When we have privilege and encounter repercussions for speaking up, we most likely have networks to fall back on. So, for those of us with privilege, how will we use that for good?

## Silence is strategic

Mateo had always wanted to be a doctor. It was his dream from the time he played with a toy stethoscope in the apartment he shared with his parents and five younger siblings. He had slogged through four years of college premed classes. He took on unpaid internships to compensate for his low test scores and strengthen his application to medical school. The day he received an acceptance letter was the happiest he'd ever been.

Now in his third year of residency, Mateo wasn't so sure—about the profession, about the system, and whether he was going to make it. He still loved caring for patients; he could even deal with the twenty-eight-hour shifts. It was the lack of respect and humanity with which his attending physician treated residents that pushed Mateo to the brink daily.

When the instructions from the attending physician didn't match the family's wishes, Mateo spoke up. "That intervention doesn't align with the patient's goals of care."

"How many patients have you actually worked with?" snapped the attending physician.

Mateo dropped the issue. Arguing wasn't worth it.

He had been told at the start of residency to treat his attending like a god: "If you cross him, it's game over." He'd let medical decisions he disagreed with go, telling himself it was part of his training; he'd tried to block out the homophobic remarks as noise. He was six months shy of finishing his residency. Without his attending's support, he would never get the fellowship he needed. After almost a decade of education and training and more than $264,000 in student debt, there was no way he was going to risk the career he had been toiling so long for.

*When I'm calling the shots, things will be different,* thought Mateo. He dreamed of the day when he was the attending and could create a team environment that welcomed different perspectives. He thought of the policy changes he would enact—standardizing systems of care, diversifying clinical trials, and removing the structural biases embedded in health care. But none of that would be possible if he didn't actually finish his residency.

For now, he bit his tongue and moved on to the next patient.

Each of us are constantly calculating how our decisions to use voice will impact our short- and long-term interests. There are times when we need to stay silent in order to stay in the game. To play by the rules long enough to get enough credibility to have influence. To play the role that's needed. Silence can allow us to solve for the things that matter most to us at one point in time.

Many of us think, *When I'm financially independent from my parents, then I'll say what I really believe.* Or *When I get promoted to the next level, then I'll stick my neck out for that cause.* But will we? We also need to be honest with ourselves—are we really playing the long game, or are we just avoiding the topic? At what point have we become complicit in perpetuating the problem rather than storing up social capital with which to fight the problem? The balance of meeting our own short- and long-term needs is complex. Asking ourselves the question "Am I really playing the long game or am I just avoiding the issue?" time and again keeps us honest about our own motivations and choices.

## Given the Costs and Benefits of Voice and Silence, What Makes Sense for Me?

In short, if the costs of choosing voice are too high, silence makes sense. If the benefits of staying silent outweigh the benefits of choosing voice, silence makes sense. But there are a few more factors that flesh out our understanding of when silence makes sense.

### Our biases

At this point, you may have observed a few factors missing from the calculation. As much as there are costs to choosing voice and benefits to staying silent, what about the costs to staying silent and the benefits of choosing voice? Why aren't we talking about those?

Sidenote: If you didn't notice, no worries. You're right on track and just proved my point.

I haven't focused our conversation on the costs of staying silent and the benefits of choosing voice because that's not where we gravitate when we're trying to figure out whether to stay silent. Instead, our brains are focused on the costs of voice and the seemingly guaranteed benefits of staying silent. We focus on these factors because of two main biases: the present bias and the self-bias.

### *Present bias*

Intellectually, we know that over time the costs of staying silent include that nothing changes, that people won't even know the challenges and frustrations we experience, and that silence perpetuates harm and violence. Many of us also know that the benefits of choosing voice can include meaningful connection, reduced isolation, and real personal and social change. But the costs of staying silent and the benefits of choosing voice are typically experienced on the time-scale of weeks, months, and years, whereas the costs of choosing voice and benefits of staying silent are experienced and enjoyed in the immediate term. If I choose voice, I have to deal with your scathing response now? No thank you. If I stay silent, I'll get my paycheck at the next pay period? Yes please. Present bias means that most of us would rather take seemingly guaranteed short-term benefits and avoidance of costs than take the gamble on long-term benefits that seem more tenuous.[26]

### *Self-bias*

As altruistic as we might think ourselves to be, it is human nature to focus on the costs and benefits that impact us individually rather than on the collective. In what Harvard Business School professor Amy Edmondson calls the voice-silence calculation, silence typically wins because individuals reap the personal benefit of staying silent by not having to incur wrath or costs of change. The benefits of staying silent are immediate, mostly guaranteed, and personal.[27] In contrast, the benefits of choosing voice are typically to benefit society or a group over time, while the costs of voice are absorbed by the individual. Since we naturally focus first on what is going to be good for us, silence makes sense.

## Our perception

From a young age, Nadeem knew that he was different than the other boys in his Pakistani immigrant community in Britain. While he was attracted to girls in his class, he was also attracted to the boys. His parents had always made it very clear that he could love whoever he wanted, so long as she was a girl who came from a good Muslim family that they knew. They would have a traditional wedding, offer a good *mehr*, and have plenty of grandchildren to make the family proud.

When Nadeem was accepted to an Ivy League graduate program in the States, his family was thrilled—having the name-brand education would mean he was set for life. It was there that Nadeem met the people he came to love most. When they were in public, onlookers often furrowed their brows at their group—all different skin colors and styles of dress. However they looked from the outside, these were people Nadeem trusted with his life. He had their backs, and they had his. Together they had built a beautiful life, with potted plants, a dinner rotation, fur babies, and a vegan Hindu Shabbat dinner every week. He knew that his parents would not approve, but their approval was no longer his goal.

It helped that the life he had built was more than four thousand miles away from where his aging parents lived. Phone calls were easy, as he could keep to the topics he knew were safe—how his career was progressing, what he had eaten for dinner, and no, he hadn't met anyone. The video calls every few months weren't bad either. After all, he knew how to dress for his family of origin. Even the annual visit home was doable, as work always needed him back after a few days. He didn't need his parents' judgment or opinion of his life.

Every few years, Nadeem's friends would ask whether he would ever tell his parents that he was pansexual. Nadeem didn't see the point. He knew that being in relationship with anyone outside his parents' worldview was already a big disappointment to his aging mother—he had watched the battle go down when one of his sisters married a White atheist. Finding the words to explain a life that was so foreign to them would take energy he didn't want to spend. Word also traveled through the community like wildfire, so it wasn't just his parents' reaction he would have to contend with, but that of every auntie and uncle they had ever been in contact with. It was easier for everyone to just focus on the PhD he had obtained and to know him as yet another person of their generation who worked too many hours in the day.

Like Nadeem, our analysis of the costs and benefits of voice or silence are based on both what is real and perceived. If Nadeem chooses to share more of his life with his parents, he will incur the real costs of needing to put energy into finding the words to explain his life to his parents. His decision is also shaped by what he perceives as the potential costs, based on his parents' reaction to his sister's marriage and his understanding of his parents' religious and cultural beliefs. While his parents could actually react differently than he anticipates, whether Nadeem chooses voice or silence is a decision for him alone to make.

Real costs are the ones that we incur when we choose voice or silence. Perceived costs are the ones we fear or anticipate based on our experiences and observations. To tell someone that it is safe to speak up or to show who they are when life experience has taught us otherwise is gaslighting.

However, if we truly want people to choose voice, we need to reduce both the real and perceived costs to choosing voice by changing how we react and respond.

If we want to change the calculus so that choosing voice makes more sense than choosing silence, we need to make it less costly to choose voice. Unless and until the benefits of choosing voice outweigh the benefits of staying silent, it simply makes sense to choose silence.

## The Difference? Agency.

When a partner at the law firm claimed that Grace was only on the team because they needed someone diverse, Grace hit her limit. She submitted her resignation without another job lined up. She could no longer work in an environment that refused to recognize her worth, used her when convenient, and diminished her. In her exit interview, she noted that the partner's xenophobic behavior was a reason for leaving.

Her friends praised her. "Wow, you're so brave. Quitting must have taken so much courage."

It's true. Quitting had taken courage. But for Grace, it wasn't just courage, but calculation. Having paid off her student debt and stashed away much of her salary over the years, Grace could afford to walk away from the colleagues and system that tore at her every day she was in the job. She had the financial means to make a choice that prioritized her emotional, mental, physical, and psychological well-being. It's not a decision that her colleague who was supporting three kids and elderly parents on the same salary and relied on the company-sponsored visa to be in the country could have made.

To choose voice, courage is necessary, but not sufficient. For some, or in some seasons of life, we simply cannot bear the costs of using our voices. So it makes sense to stay silent.

There are times when there is value and utility to silence. Our brains and bodies are wise to analyze the costs of speaking up, figure out whether we can stay whole, and determine whether and when we can stomach the costs. Whether silence is additive or oppressive depends on whether it is silence you chose or that is chosen for you.

What's the difference? Agency. Agency refers to the feeling of control over actions and consequences.[28] Having an internal locus of control allows us to exert influence that brings about change in the world. With what Stanford psychologist Albert Bandura describes as intentionality, forethought, self-reactiveness, and self-reflection, we are more able to shape the world we want to be in.[29] We decide whether we want to lend our voices to a cause or a situation, or whether it's something we don't want to take on—now or ever. The decision to choose matters.

The world is a noisy place. *You've got to speak up! Silence is violence. Whatever you're not changing, you're choosing.* While there's validity to each of those statements in different contexts, only you know what you can do—today, tomorrow, and the next day—to stay in the fight, to stay alive, to keep breathing and showing up, for yourself, your loved ones, and your community.

You're the one who has to live today and live into the future. Take the space when you need it. As an act of faith, as an act of protest, as an act of self-sustenance. Let's make whether you choose silence or voice your call.

# REFLECTION QUESTIONS

———

Take a situation where you're currently staying silent. It could be not telling your family you don't want to go on vacation with them, or not speaking up about a company policy that has an exclusionary impact. As it relates to your situation, answer the three questions to interrogate whether you want to choose silence:

## 1. What are the costs of speaking up?

Push yourself to identify: Which of these costs are known? Which of these costs are your perception? Also consider, What are the long-term costs of staying silent?

## 2. What are the benefits of staying silent?

Ask yourself: Who benefits from my silence? If you can survive, care for, and stay sufficiently whole, consider using your voice rather than staying silent.

## 3. Given the costs and benefits of voice and silence, what makes sense for me?

Disrupt your biases by examining: What long-term benefits to choosing voice might you be failing to recognize? How does your choice for voice or silence impact other people or people groups? How does your choice for voice or silence align with how you want to show up in the world?

# 4

# How We Silence Ourselves

C hristina was about to lose it.

She had hit her limit with André.

While she once would have considered him a friend, being roommates for the last six months meant that Christina had nothing but fighting words for André.

Having met through a mutual friend, André and Christina agreed to share an apartment. Their shared love for R&B music, indie films, and unsuspectingly good food made it seem like living together would be easy—maybe even fun. Sharing space helped them both afford the high rents of the city they loved. The apartment was centrally located, full of charming detail, and, unfortunately, just small enough to make everything feel a little cramped.

André was a self-admitted collector of all things. Day-to-day details and "life administration" were not his strong suit. Christina was a minimalist. Of the two of them, she was more on top of bills that needed to be split, dishes that had to be washed, and the space that needed—in her opinion—to be cleaned.

At first, having their own designated spaces within the apartment seemed to work. But as André's book collection filled the shelves and tchotchkes spilled into the common area, Christina's frustration started to brew. When he would leave the lights on all night, she would text him: "Can you turn off the lights? Our electricity bill is going to be through the roof." When she came home to fruit flies circling around a jam jar left open on the counter, she snapped a photo and said, "You have to put things away." Sometimes he would reply, sometimes he wouldn't.

Given that she worked days and he worked nights, it was easy for them to go weeks without seeing each other in person. She started leaving notes for André under his beloved cat magnet on the refrigerator that said "Please clean up your things" and "Remember: this is our shared space." She vented to their mutual friend, who told her to give André a break. After all, he was still reeling from his last breakup.

"Just be the bigger person," she told herself as she tried to shrug things off. "It's not that huge of a deal." But just as quickly, she would think, "What's so wrong with wanting to live in a sanitary place? This is my home too." The times they saw each other in person were so rare that when they were together Christina tried to keep things pleasant. They talked about the sweltering summer heat and how good the laksa was at the new hole-in-the-wall restaurant. Wanting to preserve the friendship, Christina didn't say anything about the state of their space or the resentment she felt. After all this time, she was worried that if she did say something, her thoughts would come out with a vengeance and vehemence she didn't intend.

She tried to keep the peace.

LIKE CHRISTINA, WHETHER WE WANT TO SHARE AN IDEA OR IN-novation, push back against a strategy we're convinced won't work, or have a hard conversation with a friend, speaking up can be costly. When deciding whether to speak up, we need to figure out whether and how to say something. Most of us are also anticipating and calculating the emotional and relational impacts the comment will have on the other person, ourselves, and the systems in which we live and work.

In a decade of consulting with professionals to handle difficult conversations, I've noticed a particular dynamic. Very few people are as clear as they think they are. Whether it's sugarcoating, self-censoring, or hedging, most people are not as unfiltered or direct as they might be if there were no costs to how we show up. That's not to mention the 45 percent of Americans—myself included—who regularly self-censor for fear that expressing their view will isolate and alienate them from others.[1]

What we say—and what we don't—impacts the quality of work assignments we receive, the reputation we build, and, at worst, whether we have a livelihood or enjoy physical safety. In this chapter, I outline behavioral traps we fall into that undercut the strength and impact of our voices, often without realizing we're undercutting ourselves. I shed light on things people tend to do, so you can notice whether they are things you do—and whether doing so serves you.

## IS IT THEM OR IS IT YOU? LIKELY BOTH.

There's no doubt that the relationships and environment that other people create influence the degree of psychological safety we experience and our perception of whether it's worth it to speak up. And yet it's useful to interrogate whether there's anything we can change on our end, independent of whether others change.

Wait, why are we looking at ourselves when it's so clearly their fault for not creating a safe environment? For shutting us down time and again? For supporting us in word, but not in deed? Because we have far more control over the things we do and the inputs we make to a relational system than we have over others. Changing behavior requires people to disrupt habits while cultivating a new set of actions—and doing so typically takes longer than we prefer.[2] It can take anywhere from 18 to 254 days for someone to form a new habit, and an average of 66 days for a new behavior to become automatic.[3]

To be clear, asking what we can change doesn't mean letting other people off the hook. It's making sure we utilize every possible lever for change, including the ones over which we ourselves have more control. What are the things, if any, we could change, without anyone else needing to change, that would make a difference in whether my voice is heard, my needs are met, and I am known? If those unilateral changes exist, it is likely worth giving them a try. After all, doing something different ourselves is often a whole lot easier than trying to get someone else to change.

I'm not saying that it's all on us, because it's not. But in the spirit of leaving no stone unturned, let's at least consider what we can do, since waiting for others to choose to change is a far harder and typically less fruitful exercise.

## We Assume Our Voices Don't Matter

The words *innovation, collaboration,* and *creativity* hung on the sage-green walls of the meeting room, as if having the words as part of the décor would manifest the concepts into reality. The meeting was supposed to be generative—where new artists shared their ideas and people of all levels could offer insights on the film's storyboard. But Vinay noticed himself staying silent. He was a junior member of the art department. He wasn't an expert. He had been at the studio precisely three months—long enough to observe that regardless of what ideas people offered in these meetings, Jeff, the creative director, ended up doing whatever he wanted. Even as others asked, "Vinay, what do you think?" he kept quiet, assuming that he didn't have anything to add.

When his manager asked Vinay in a one-on-one check-in why he wasn't contributing in the storyboard meetings, Vinay was confused. "I'm the newest person in the room and low on the pecking order. Isn't it my job to observe? I wouldn't want to step on someone's toes or turf." The conversation was illuminating for Vinay's manager, who saw things differently. Vinay's manager, and the studio as a whole, held the belief that everyone's perspective mattered. That regardless of how long someone had been with the studio, they could see elements that could make the story better.

"Even if you aren't a twenty-year veteran filmmaker, your unique lens on the world and human experience still help bring the characters to life in a realistic way," his manager explained. "In fact, the fresh eyes you bring to the mix helps the studio from getting stuck in the same way of doing things."

Comparing his own perspective with his manager's, Vinay was struck by the difference and, if he was honest, a little skeptical of what he heard. He'd long followed the unspoken rules of hierarchy, believing that the more senior someone was, the more they had to offer. What his manager was describing was alluring, but also a completely different paradigm from what Vinay knew. Playing to those new rules would mean he'd have to take some risks in sharing his thoughts and take a different stance in those meetings. He would have to look critically at the storyboard rather than trying to observe the group dynamics and figure out how things worked around here. His last employer had drilled into him that new people didn't know anything; they were blank slates. This studio's view of the world that everyone had valuable perspective would take some getting used to.

"If the studio really values all perspectives on the storyboard, why does it seem like Jeff ends up doing what he wants anyways?" asked Vinay. Vinay's manager didn't have a great answer for that, but he was able to recall different times when Jeff and other directors had changed things as a result of peoples' perspectives. That directors had taken on feedback was information that Vinay didn't have. And Vinay's observations were a useful mirror to look at whether there was a disconnect between what the studio aspired to and how people—Vinay included—might be experiencing the culture and norms.

We each hold different assumptions about the value of our voice and the unspoken rules about who gets to speak and what happens as a result of it:

> *My voice doesn't matter.*
>
> *Speaking up won't help.*
>
> *Only experts get to speak.*

And these assumptions can drive our behaviors. Known as the cofounder of organizational development, business theorist and professor Chris Argyris introduced the concept of double-loop learning in the 1970s. Single-loop learning looks only at the feedback from an action to review a decision. Double-loop learning questions the internalized assumptions that drive the decisions in the first place. If we really want to change the results we're getting, we need to look not only at the behaviors that led to those results, but at the assumptions behind them.[4] For example, if I stayed silent in a meeting and things didn't go my way, single-loop learning would say that my choices going forward are speak up or stay silent—neither of which feels doable or satisfying. But if I look at the assumptions that made me stay silent, I'd realize that I don't think it's worth my time to speak up because I'm convinced that managers never listen. If we can identify the assumptions, we can check and challenge them to see whether they still serve and support the people we want to be. Until we pause to identify and interrogate them, the assumptions remain the invisible forces that drive us.

Being new to a place or relationship can be disorienting. How do things work around here? What is the right thing to do? What's going to keep me safe? What's going to work here? In failing to recognize and challenge the assumptions we hold, we draw conclusions about who, what, where, when, and how we can talk about things, based on our past experiences. While those assumptions may have been valid or useful in other contexts, they may not be representative of the here and now. If we don't stop and challenge the assumptions, we perpetuate the ways that they silence us.

We know that using our voices is important for us individually, for the people around us, and for the world. But over time, we start to assume our voices don't matter.

How does that happen?

## We focus too much on others' expectations

For people whose parents moved to a different country to provide "a better future" for their children, it's usually clear what you're supposed to be doing in life—make good on your parents' sacrifice by making the most of the opportunities before you. Much of the time, that means getting a job that pays well and attaining socio-economic security. The question to answer is not what do I want to do, but what *should* I be doing? Choosing a career, spouse, or life is not about pursuing passions or living your truth, but instead about living up to the expectations others have of you.

Understanding others' expectations is part of being a considerate family member, coworker, and human being. But many of us have overrotated to the point that everything is about other people. As a result, we forget that our own needs and preferences matter. Finding our voices is an opportunity to recalibrate and consider: What matters to me? What do I want to put energy, time, and effort toward?

## We give in to peer pressure

After years of working as a professional commercial baker, Gabby started her own shop. All she wanted to do was bring the joys of sugar, butter, and flour to the world. But as a small business owner, Gabby found herself wearing every hat—innovator, marketer, janitor, accountant.

After a few features in different newspapers and blogs, Gabby's business took off. She was able to add to her team. Remembering what it was like to work three jobs just to make rent, and not wanting others to have to do the same, she decided she would pay above the normal hourly rate for the industry. Despite hiring new people,

Gabby was still feeling overwhelmed. Her brother suggested she talk with a business adviser, someone who knew nothing about baking but plenty about business. The adviser had some useful ideas about training other people to do the labor-intensive custom decorating, and rearranging the storefront so that it would be more inviting.

"As a small business trying to grow, you should be investing money back into the business," the adviser told her. "You can get away with paying people market rate." He argued that because she was a small operation, she was justified in paying less than a larger bakery.

The advice was tempting. Having more cash would certainly make the other changes easier. Gabby could hire more people if she paid less. She could pay the first installment on the bill to have the linoleum floors replaced.

Gabby was torn. She knew the hustle of being in the food industry. Having her own shop was supposed to be about getting to do things her way. Just because she could pay less didn't mean that she wanted to. She had wanted to run things differently. To make her own mark on the industry.

Her brother was quick to remind her, "You're a baker, not a businessperson."

Gabby listened. With her next hire, she lowered the hourly rate, telling herself that it was the right business decision. The adviser had said so. Months later, her team members came to her. "Why is Rachel paid less than us? We do the same job. We thought we could trust you." Gabby felt like she had been caught red-handed. She mumbled the business adviser's line about how her bakery was smaller, but even she wasn't persuaded. Not only had she created inequity on the team, she had compromised her own values and what she stood for.

When we repeatedly give in to pressure from others to act a certain way, we diminish the value of our preferences and our sense of voice. We silence ourselves when we go along with what others want for us, even though what they want doesn't seem right to us. Over time, taking on advice that doesn't sit well with us can dull our instincts to the point where we no longer think they're valuable. We start to assume our voice doesn't matter.

## We value sameness over uniqueness

Mimicry—the unconscious tendency to imitate—is a well-documented phenomenon among humans. When we depend on, feel close to, or want to be liked by others, we unconsciously mimic their behavior.[5] People tend to have more positive judgments about, be more willing to help, and say yes to people who mimic them.[6] So much so that books on influence recommend imitation as a way for humans to create a good impression and have positive relationships with others.[7]

The effects of mimicry make sense—after all, there is an ease to engaging with people who act like us. Mimicking what others are already doing seems less risky than treading new ground, because there is already a track record for their behaviors. When entering a new workplace or family system, taking time to observe the existing system is wise. This is especially true when you hold subordinated identities because your place in a system is already more tenuous.

At the same time, mimicry—particularly being rewarded for our mimicry—dulls our unique way of showing up in the world. We start to wonder if our worth and effectiveness are tied up in how we imitate others. If our worth comes from our sameness, why would we even begin to think that our own voices matter? But without difference, learning and innovation are impossible.

When I first started in corporate education, I mimicked what the founders of our firm did. After all, they were senior faculty at Harvard and authors of a *New York Times* bestselling book. The way they developed business, worked with clients, and taught workshops had a proven track record of success. There was already a stamp of approval on their way of doing things. I learned to describe concepts and engage clients as they did, so much so that one client noted we had the same enunciation. As I understood it, my job was to channel their voice in order to scale their impact.

When people requested me for client work, I thought it was because I was a good imitation of our founders, but at a lower rate. One day, a client said she didn't want a founder for the work. In fact, she wanted me because of the heart and insight I brought.

The idea that someone would want me for me, not because I was a decent imitation of someone else, is still something I'm wrapping my head around. It's still a little surreal to me that I—a unique individual—have something to say. That my voice might matter.

Slowly but surely, I am choosing to embrace rather than hide my uniqueness. I'm starting to assume that my voice matters. Given the agency, ability, and opportunity to make decisions, what will *my* approach be?

## We Self-Censor

*I wish they would edit themselves.*

*I don't want to be like* those *people.*

*They suck all the energy out of the room.*

These are the types of things we think to ourselves as we not-so-secretly judge the overtalkers and oversharers around us.

Our fears of being overbearing or that we'd dominate a conversation aren't unfounded. In a typical six-person meeting, more than 60 percent of the talking is done by just two people.[8] The link between speaking time and perceived authority is so well established that some researchers call it the babble hypothesis of leadership. Consciously or unconsciously, people speak to try to demonstrate leadership. And many people interpret speaking time as a sign of leadership or leadership potential.[9]

But if you're concerned about coming across as overbearing, it's more likely that you're far from being overbearing. After all, you're aware enough to even be concerned in the first place. Instead, you're likely censoring yourself in an overcorrection that undercuts your ability to advocate for yourself and contribute to the world.

Researchers have defined self-censorship as withholding one's true opinion from an audience perceived to disagree with that opinion.[10] Why do we self-censor? Because if we're used to being censored by others, it doesn't feel all that different to do it to ourselves. Because we aren't confident that the costs of speaking up outweigh the benefits. Because we debate ourselves out of saying something. What often seems like a split-second intuitive decision leads us to the conclusion that it's not worth the costs to speak up.

For years, Patreeya struggled to figure out a way to make her relationship with her mother work. Her mom had sacrificed so much, working three jobs and leaving their extended family in Thailand so that Patreeya could have different opportunities in life. Without her mom, Patreeya wouldn't be where she was. But Patreeya felt as if she had no control over her own life and no freedom to explore the different options that her education and environment afforded her. Every conversation seemed to center on how Patreeya could improve, or what she was doing wrong or needed to do.

To tell her mom to give her space would be to seem ungrateful.

So Patreeya nodded—even as she rolled her eyes during the phone call—and said nothing when her mom nagged her about this or that. Whenever Patreeya called her mom, she would hang up the phone feeling discouraged and depleted. The list of what needed to change about their dynamic was so clear in her head: I need space to make my own mistakes. I need you to recognize that I'm no longer nine years old. I need you to recognize the things I'm doing well. I need to know that you'll love and accept me, whatever I do.

But Patreeya didn't feel like she could say anything.

After all, she didn't want to come across as selfish or demanding.

Perhaps you can spot what's flawed about the arguments that swirled in Patreeya's mind. Like Patreeya, we come up with and anticipate rebuttals to avoid dealing with the issue—even though the rebuttals may or may not be the other person's actual response. We get stuck in what we experience as a dilemma. Patreeya denied her own needs and became increasingly bitter and distant because she couldn't get what she needed, in part because of her own self-imposed ban on saying what she wanted and needed from her mom.

So what can we do instead? Share the dilemma instead of letting the dilemma be a reason not to say anything. Patreeya could say to her mom, "Mom, I love you and want us to have a strong relationship. I'm so grateful for what you've sacrificed for me. It is also really hurtful to constantly hear what you think I'm doing wrong, without hearing what you think I'm doing well or right. Can we change the balance of what we talk about in our calls?"

"But" has long been known as the "great eraser." Connecting two thoughts with "but" has the impact of erasing the thought that precedes it. Instead, consider adopting an "and" stance; using "and" to connect thoughts allows us to share the tension we're experiencing and illuminate the natural complexity of life. Because we—and the world—are indeed complex.

*I love you, and you are driving me crazy.*

*I'm excited about the client prospect and daunted by the task before us.*

*I want to support the plan, and I have concerns about the approach.*

Both—or all of—the statements can be true at the same time. The different thoughts are part of the complexity of being human. When we edit out parts of the complexity, we are less complete versions of ourselves. We withhold information that is essential for developing holistic and sustainable solutions. Censoring means being unidimensional in a multicolored, multidimensional world.

Sometimes we agonize about whether to speak up, taking so much time to decide that the moment in the meeting has passed. Other times, silence is so habitual that we don't even realize we've made an implicit decision to stay silent in the moment. Furthermore, our brains make up their minds up to ten seconds before we realize we've made a decision. By looking at brain activity, researchers can predict what choice people are going to make before they themselves are even aware.[11] Where might you be so used to censoring yourself that you don't even realize you could choose a different way?

## We Mitigate Our Speech

I had the good fortune to travel with my brother the summer after I graduated college. We bought Eurail passes and sought out the most affordable hostels. I remember my stomach rumbling with hunger and asking him, "Are you hungry?" To which he replied, "Nope." And on we walked.

I fumed for a while, upset that he wasn't considering me.

Why couldn't we look for food now?

Why did we always have to do things his way?

Why couldn't he read my mind and know that I was hungry?

I swirled in silent annoyance before realizing that there was no reason (other than my own personal wish that everyone around me would read my mind and cater to my needs in just the way that I'd prefer without my ever having to articulate things) that he would know that "Are you hungry?" actually meant "I'm hungry, can we go find some food?" Or better yet, "I'm hungry, I'm going to get food."

In hindsight, it's easy to see the gap between the message I intended to convey and the words that came out of my mouth. Seeing that gap also sheds light on why my brother wasn't getting the message. How often is there a gap between what we intend to say and what we actually say?

Author Malcolm Gladwell popularized the term *mitigated speech*, defining it as any attempt to downplay or sugarcoat the meaning of what is being said.[12] We soften the force or scope of what we say in order to make it easier for the other person to hear. Linguists have long studied mitigated speech, particularly between individuals of perceived power differences.[13] Women and people of color have learned to mitigate our speech to make ourselves more palatable to people in power—and then get dinged for not being as clear as we need to be.

Why would there be a power difference between me and my brother? Because I grew up the youngest child of a family steeped in implicit patriarchy. As much as my parents tried to ensure parity between the two of us in our life in the United States, the preference for sons runs deep in Chinese culture. For thousands of years,

Chinese families wanted sons over daughters because men traditionally had more earning capacity than women, could carry on the family name, add to the family labor force, provide security for parents'
old age, and perform ancestral rites.[14] Even if we actively tried to
combat the preference, I still internalized the embedded defer-
ence across gender and age. But recognition of my mitigated speech
helped unravel and preserve what was otherwise a unique opportunity for sibling bonding and seeing the world together.

Looking back, my exchange with my brother seems silly. But the
realization was significant for me. Where else had I fallen into the
trap of mitigated speech? How many other times had I been frustrated that people couldn't read my mind when I hadn't given them
much to read?

Now raising a toddler, I'm often saying to my son, "Can you use
your words?" But the question works for adults too. Can we use our
words? Can we get enough clarity on what we are actually asking for
and then say it out loud—to the person who needs to hear it? Using
my words requires giving myself permission to state my own needs.
My being hungry and doing something about it didn't need to depend on whether my brother was also hungry at the time. In group-
oriented cultures, it can seem strange or selfish to advocate and
solve for our own needs. But the reality is, we are going to have different needs than other people do. It is on us to be able to identify
and decide how to articulate them.

So how do we communicate our needs? It can be helpful to look
at the different degrees of mitigation in how we communicate—the
most indirect being a hint, the most direct being a command.[15] Each
level of directness has utility, particularly when communicating
across cultures, and the different levels can be combined for desired
effect. Below is an analysis of the different levels of directness in-

volved in mitigated speech, using the example of my wanting to get food while traveling with my brother.

| LEVEL OF DIRECTNESS | WHAT IT IS | WHAT IT SOUNDS LIKE |
| --- | --- | --- |
| Command | Tell people what to do. | We're getting food now. |
| Proposal | Endorse an option. | Let's get food now. |
| Suggestion | Put forth an option. | What if we get food now ... |
| Question | Ask a question. | Are you hungry? |
| Observation | Make an observation. | It's been a while since we ate. |
| Hint | Indicate indirectly. | Food here is different than at home. |

Cultural contexts and our roles within those contexts often call for different levels of directness. This is why Americans are often perceived as being rude in France, or those who live in Iowa can bristle at a New Yorker's directness. At work, if you're the most junior person in a meeting, commanding a senior leader isn't likely to go over well. If you're meeting your significant other's parents for the first time for dinner at their house, you're likely best served making observations and asking questions than trying to command them in their own home. At the same time, if you're not getting traction, that might be because your style of communication is out of sync with the norms of the culture and the context you're in.

When haven't you been as clear as you could have been? When might it help you to expand the options of how you might communicate? Bottom line? Choose the level of directness that you think best supports your purpose in the moment.

If you're still having a hard time being direct and advocating for yourself, two mental hacks can help us get much-needed self-advocacy. If we're trained to think about the collective good rather than individual good, we can prioritize our individual good by realizing our own well-being is actually a collective good. When traveling with my brother, my not being hangry is in our collective interest. I am going to be a better version of myself if I'm fed. I'm going to be better company, less resentful, and able to contribute to enjoying the trip. My naming my needs allows us to solve for those needs, which means a better trip for everyone.

I wish having needs was enough to get me to name and meet them. That I wouldn't have to link my individual needs to a collective good to see that they have value. But when entrapped by the weight of the dominant paradigm, I'm happy to use a mental hack to get to the same outcome of meeting my needs.

The second mental hack is a mindset shift. Classic negotiation theory says that every party to the negotiation has a set of interests. If I am impacted by this decision, then I, too, have a set of interests, needs, goals, hopes, and concerns we collectively need to solve for. We're not solving for my interests because I'm special, or because I'm needy, but because negotiation is the process of solving for the interests of all the parties. Everyone involved in the negotiation needs to solve for my needs, just as I would solve for and care for theirs. Can I get clear on what my needs are? Apparently in the moment it was both food and to be known.

Researcher Brené Brown popularized the slogan "Clear is kind."[16] Can we negotiate ourselves to rewrite the narrative so being clear is kind, and being unclear is unkind? Then can we actually be clear? To hedge and sugarcoat less? To notice the disconnect between the things we intend to say, and what we actually say? We can't control how people hear the things we say, but we do have control over what we actually say.

# We Never Speak in the First Place

In addition to the question of whether we've said things as clearly as we need or intend, there's the more fundamental question of whether we actually said it to the person themselves.

When we're upset with something, we tend to vent to people we trust. We stew on the issue. We fume in silence. At times, we play and replay the situation.

The challenge with memory is that as we describe and gripe about something to *everyone else* in our lives, our memories start to rewrite history. We start to believe that we might have actually had the conversation with the person even if we haven't.

Psychologists call this the illusory truth effect. The more a statement is repeated, the more likely we are to believe it is true. Even highly implausible statements become more plausible with enough repetition.[17] One explanation for this effect is that it's easier for our brains to process and understand repeated statements. The ease with which something is processed is used as a signal for truth.

This effect is both deeply disturbing and reason to pause. Repeating misinformation doesn't make it true but does make it more likely to be believed. It becomes our truth, unless we stop to pause and ask: Did I actually say it to that person? I've described my version of events to everyone else—my friends, family, neighbor, even the random grocery-store worker when they asked how my day was. But did I actually say it to the person who needs to hear it? No.

The tricks our brains play on us are related to defense mechanisms. The most adaptive defenses are those that allow for gratification. We don't like distorted reality, so we change reality—not always consciously. Venting is a form of instant gratification that can displace the actual feelings caused by the conflict.[18]

For years, Tara's company had a full-time employee create all the company's graphics. Having a full-time employee do that work always seemed like a poor use of resources to Tara, especially when the person doing the work didn't have a background or a knack for doing the work. To Tara, the graphics were an embarrassment. She knew freelance designers who could do the work faster, better, and for a lower hourly rate than what she assumed the company was paying her colleague.

Tara knew that outsourcing the work was a business decision that would save the company time and money, and result in visual assets that would play better in the market. But whenever she thought about making the suggestion, she dismissed the idea. Her design-challenged colleague was so passionate about their work. The one time her colleague had asked Tara what she thought about the graphics she mumbled something about the design not being her taste. Seeing the crestfallen look on the colleague's face, she quickly followed up with, "But I'm not the decision maker here." As someone returning to the workforce after raising three kids, Tara didn't want to do anything that would make her seem less of a team player. So time and again, she let the thought go.

When friends would ask Tara whether the company had moved on from its clip-art phase, she'd shake her head and say that the company wasn't willing to do it. Every time she looked at a company graphic, she cringed and told herself it wasn't her battle to fight.

Instead, she vented to friends about how backward the company was. About how the decision to let this one person work on a pet project reeked of nepotism, to the detriment of the company's public image. She griped about it. But she never made the suggestion to outsource graphic design directly to the leaders who could do something about it. She assumed what leadership's response would be instead of letting them respond for themselves.

It's not unlike many workplace dynamics, where individuals complain to their peers and coworkers about an issue. They might even raise the issue with the person's manager. But rarely do people talk directly with the individual about the issue itself. At some level it's more comfortable to keep the narrative in your head, as that's where you have control over it. It also means that others don't have the opportunity to defy the character you've made them out to be in your head or to choose a different way.

A few years later, a young White male colleague joined Tara's team. One of his first suggestions was that the company outsource graphic design to a freelancer rather than use full-time resources for the task, as it would save the company time and energy. Leadership agreed.

It is one thing if we're saying something but others are choosing not to hear it. It's another if they're not hearing it because we're not saying it.

There are plenty of cases of the former, but if you find yourself in the latter, actually making the suggestion or sharing the idea with the people who can do something about it is a key step to increasing the likelihood that they might hear it.

IF WE BREAK COMMUNICATION DOWN VERY PRACTICALLY, THERE ARE only a few possible failure points we need to guard against: whether we say something, how we say it, who we say it to, and whether people hear it. We have the least control over whether people will hear us, but we have far more control over the first three possible failure points. In this chapter, we've examined the ways that our internalized assumptions, self-censorship, mitigated speech, and mental tricks can silence us—even without realizing it. I challenge you to reflect on whether these are patterns you've fallen into as part of the silence you learned and experiment with disrupting those patterns. After all, we have more control over whether we're silencing ourselves than we do over how others silence us.

At the end of the day, we may choose to be more direct and less mitigated. We may say what needs to be said to the person to whom it needs to be said. And they still may not hear it—because of their own assumptions or biases around someone who is a different age, a different race, or someone like you or me. Similarly, we might not hear everyone or everything—a challenge we're going to tackle in the next chapter.

# REFLECTION QUESTIONS

---

What assumptions do you hold about
the value of your voice? Where along the way
might you have lost your sense of voice?

With whom and in what contexts do
you censor yourself?

What levels of directness do you tend to use?
How might you broaden your range to increase
the likelihood people hear you?

# 5

# How We Silence Others

We can't look at silence without also considering how we've silenced others.

You may be thinking, *Wait, I don't have anything to do with the problem. I'm the one who's been silenced. I'm the last person who would ever intend to silence someone else. I'm a good person. Sure, there are people who shut others down, but I'm not one of those people.*

To this I say, most of us *are* good people. And we still—intentionally or unintentionally—shut others down. Me included.

You can be a good person and still have someone in your life feel unseen, unknown, unheard, and undervalued by you.

You can be an impactful leader and still not know how to manage employees who look, sound, and work differently than you do.

You can want to build a world where people have the candid conversations that stem off crises and support growth and still have people tiptoeing around and withholding information from you.

You can be trustworthy and others still might not trust that you won't bite their heads off.

Many of us have the best of intentions. We are working hard to foster healthy teams and create loving families and nourishing communities. Hearing that our best efforts are falling short can be discouraging and demotivating. This is when silence can be an illusively attractive option. In maintaining the status quo, silence offers predictability, stability, and a sense of control in a world that often feels out of our control. If I don't hear that what I'm doing isn't landing well with you, I can more easily assume all is good. If no one says they see things differently, then there's no reason to think that there might be a different way to see things or that change is necessary. Silence affords us the luxury of ignorance.

As humans, we focus (or fixate) on the times that people have silenced us, when we've been told to shut up or we've felt shot down. It is human nature to remember the places and spaces where we've been hurt, and to shy away from the places and spaces where we've hurt others. Our brains deprioritize the coding and retrieval of unwanted memories in order to help keep us functional.[1] Yale psychologists and economists have found that people tend to remember themselves being better to others than they actually were. Our brains adapt our memories so we can avoid feeling bad about our own behavior. Misremembering the moments when we weren't our finest is one way of maintaining our moral self-image.[2]

Silence from people and silencing people means I don't have to see or reckon with the potentially ugly parts of myself. But if we want a world that supports people, those are the parts of ourselves we need to see.

In this chapter, I invite us to lower our guard. Given the many roles we play and relationships we hold, we can both be silenced and be silencing people at any one time.

In the next few sections, I'll identify patterns that are so common we call them human nature. I'll elucidate the less-than-ideal impacts we're having on the people around us so those same people don't have to do the emotional labor of educating us about why we're missing the mark, while reeling from our missing the mark. As you read, ask yourself: Where might I have fallen into these patterns? Am I doing this right now? What could I do instead?

I'll try to write with as much compassion and clarity as possible. My hope is that this awareness of patterns becomes a catalyst for personal reflection and conscious action.

Below are patterns we fall into that have the impact of silencing the very people we often want to support.

## We Underestimate the Challenge

Steve had hired Maribel because he saw her raw talent. Her new role was arguably a bit of a stretch for her existing skill set, but Steve was committed to giving people opportunities to grow. He personally hated being micromanaged, so he made sure to give people on his team lots of space to do things their way. He also made clear that if there was ever anything they needed, he was all ears.

Maribel wanted to be successful in her new role and had so much to be grateful for. The company had taken a chance on her. The job came with benefits, paid vacation, and, eventually, a pension. She was determined to prove that they hadn't made a mistake hiring her. Yet being the first member of her family to go to college meant that she was constantly unsure how the corporate world worked. When she visited her family on weekends, the friends she grew up with mocked her. *How's that fancy new job? Don't go thinking you're too good for us now.* Being in a world different from the one she grew up in was alienating. If she didn't succeed at the role, she couldn't really go back.

Maribel watched as people who joined the organization after her got promoted. Somehow, they were getting roles and opportunities that she hadn't even known about. Where were the job postings? How were people finding out about these things? It was like there was a secret network that she didn't have access to.

Her annual performance review was coming up. The review was her chance to find out how they really thought she was doing and to ask why others were getting promoted before her. She was determined not to waste her shot.

In the conversation, Steve asked her if there was anything she would change about her current role.

*C'mon, Maribel. Just say it!* she thought. But when she tried, the words got stuck in her throat. Her palms were sweaty, her face flushed, and her mind went blank.

The words had come out relatively smoothly when she had practiced what she wanted to say in the mirror. She wanted to know whether she was the only one who worked nights and weekends. She wanted to know why she hadn't been paid overtime for those hours. She wanted to know why people were getting promoted and she wasn't. But all those thoughts were stuck inside her.

For Maribel, asking for more was difficult for so many reasons. Maribel's family had taught her not to question authority, to be grateful for every opportunity, and that hard work would be rewarded. She trusted that people who had been around longer and who were in positions with more influence would make good choices on behalf of the organization and the people they employed.

As Maribel shook her head no, Steve moved on in the conversation. He assumed that her silence meant all was good. After all, he had asked the question and she had said no.

Like Steve, we silence people by failing to realize just how hard it is for some people to speak up. If we don't struggle with speaking up, it might seem odd to us that it could be difficult for others. If we've never felt the need to wait for an invitation before speaking, it is not intuitive that others might be waiting for the invitation. People who grew up with their voices being celebrated and efforts rewarded have different data points than those who didn't. We have examples of when we spoke up, people heard us, and there was an acceptance or even changes as a result of our speaking up. Not everyone has those experiences in their data set. As a result, we underestimate the challenge of saying something or we forget it's a challenge at all. We don't have empathy for the challenge, and we don't do anything to make it easier.

Two thirds of professionals surveyed reported that they are never or rarely scary to those junior to them.[3] Yet in a different study, six out of ten people reported being too intimidated to go to their boss or manager with an issue.[4] While the math isn't perfect, the studies show a disconnect between how we see ourselves and how others see us. We're sitting around thinking, *I'm the kindest, most welcoming, least intimidating person I know.* And yet others don't share those perceptions of us, especially across lines of power. While the disconnect may be frustrating to realize, it is also an invitation to ask: How are we really coming across to people? What could we do differently to have the impact we intend? What can we do to avoid underestimating the challenge?

A lot. We can remember how hard it can be for people to speak. We can ask people how we can support them. We can invite their voices in regularly. We can affirm people's contributions when they share their perspectives. We can make clear which avenues are available for raising issues so that the individual doesn't have to do the work of figuring it out. We can build trust over time so rather than someone seeing us as the culmination of all the worst nightmares they've had about someone in our role, they can see us as people.

## We Say We Want Input When We Really Don't

As a teenager, Nathan was the program assistant at a science camp for middle schoolers. After each day's program, the director would ask each staff member to share one thing that worked well and one thing they would want the team to do differently. While some staff members shrugged through this part of the day and halfheartedly mumbled answers, Nathan put a lot of thought into what he would offer, especially on what the team could do differently. He knew he wanted to be a teacher when he grew up, and his family had taught him to do everything with sincerity. He noted that some campers felt put on the spot when called on during activities, so he recommended the director give advance warning about when they might be called on so campers could think ahead about what they wanted to say. The director nodded at his suggestion and put it on the list. But the next day, the director continued to call on campers without warning. At the end of the day, Nathan again made the same suggestion. Still there was no change.

One of the other assistants said to him, "Geez, Nathan, chill out. Let it go. It's not that big a deal." Nathan had learned his lesson. The next time he was asked what he thought, he wasn't going to invest the time to come up with suggestions. Apparently, input wasn't really welcome or valued at the camp.

Whether at work, in our communities, or across the dinner table, there is pressure to be inclusive. We're supposed to invite perspective and build consensus when we can. Too often, we make the representations about our openness we think we're supposed to make, rather than being honest about how open we actually are. We confuse valuing an individual with having to value their opinion on a particular topic. At best, the disconnect leads to confusion. At worst, the disconnect leads to manipulation or being lured into a false sense of security. We silence people when we pretend to want their input, and even invite input because that's what we think we should do. But if we're not really open to the input or not in a part of the process where we can engage, inviting additional input muddies the waters for everyone, confuses the process, and undercuts the level of trust in the relationship.

Listening to others doesn't mean that we have to adopt every suggestion. But if we're going to ask for input and not implement the suggestion, we need to set the expectation that not all suggestions are going to be implemented. And for those that aren't adopted, we need to communicate a reason for why not, or why not now. In the absence of conversation and communication, people tend to assume futility. There are few things more demotivating than exerting effort to use your voice and having the message disappear into the void.

## Three buckets

One of the leadership constructs I use most in coaching is that of the three buckets. Whether meal planning at home or project planning at work, every endeavor involves people in three buckets: those who decide, those to consult, and those who need to be informed.[5] The intent of the buckets is to increase clarity in communication, collaboration, and teamwork. Clear expectations about who will decide, consult, and be informed allows everyone to know where to spend energy. Try as we might, not everyone can fall in the decide bucket. Consensus does not work for everything.[6] Clarity about who makes the decision does. As much as people might want to give and get input, it's also impossible to consult everyone about everything. As a result, everyone who doesn't fall in the decide or consult bucket goes in the inform bucket.

| BUCKET | EXPECTATION |
| --- | --- |
| Decide | • Make the decision.<br>• Communicate reasoning to others. |
| Consult | • Share candid perspective and data.<br>• Advocate for the outcome you think best.<br>• Accept and respect end decision. |
| Inform | • Listen to the decision maker.<br>• Decide whether to negotiate or give feedback. |

A prime example of the three buckets is what role people play in decisions about whom you date. Prior to meeting the person who is now my spouse, my parents had never met anyone I dated. That's because when I told my parents I was dating someone, the inevitable barrage of questions would come. Who are they? How old are they? What do they do? How do you know they are who they say they are? It was easier (but not necessarily wiser) to say that I wasn't seeing anyone.

When venting about their concerns to a colleague, she said something I'll never forget. "Who you date isn't your parents' decision. It's not like dating is a team sport." Even in the moment, I recall saying, "Oh, you clearly aren't from my family."

In my culture, dating is very much a team sport. If my family didn't like who I was dating, the relationship was doomed. It had never occurred to me that dating might be an individual sport.

As I found myself frustrated with how people in my life were showing up, I had a realization. If I was choosing to share about my life, it would help if I was clear about what role I was hoping people very invested in my life would play—and explore how my expectations about the role they'd play compares with the role they'd want to play.

Is dating an individual or team sport? It depends. If we use the three buckets, are my parents (or any other vested stakeholders) actually joint decision makers in who I date or marry? Are they consulted? Or are they just informed? Drawing the distinction in roles would have helped us all avoid the friction we experienced and help me better understand how to interpret their inevitable comments that the people I dated were clearly wrong for me.

Trying to listen to everyone about everything is an impossible task. Friction comes when there is misalignment in which bucket we each think we're in, including what and how we communicate. If we have clarity on which bucket we're in, we can negotiate explicitly to be in a different bucket or better manage our expectations of what role we'll play. Either way, everyone has a clearer idea of where and how to invest their energy.

We silence people when we aren't realistic, honest, and truthful with ourselves and with them about the input we want. If you don't actually want to hear what they have to say or aren't at a part of the process where you can engage with more input, don't say, "I'm all ears." Or "Come to me with anything." It might make you feel like a good person to be able to make these statements, but if you can't deliver on the openness, you're making things worse. Don't set expectations you can't fulfill.

## We Control the Narrative

As a child, Leon was slow to speak. While pediatricians expect kids to speak about fifty words by the time they are two years old, Leon had only ever uttered a handful of words. The doctors were concerned and recommended speech therapy. The culprit? Leon's older brother. Four years older than Leon, Yianni anticipated and translated Leon's grunts. When someone asked Leon, "What do you want?" Yianni replied. At first, it was endearing, and their parents praised Yianni for watching out for his brother. But turns out, the way that Yianni could best help his brother was to let Leon speak for himself.

Leon's not alone. Children with older siblings show lesser language skills than those without older siblings. Researchers attribute the difference to older siblings competing for parental attention and speaking on behalf of their younger siblings.[7]

The pattern of speaking on someone else's behalf plays out regularly among adults. The communications team handles messaging. The leader speaks on behalf of the group. We are sworn to secrecy because our friends don't want other people to know what's really going on. While getting a consistent narrative is important for cohesion, stock price, and efficacy, controlling the narrative can also have the impact of silencing others—sometimes intentionally. We need cohesive narratives. But is there space to express different experiences and perspectives rather than just toeing a party line? Failing to question or invite additions to the dominant narrative isn't just destructive because it squashes voices, it's also leaving out data that could otherwise be useful.

Labor economist and researcher Nadiya had submitted a short bio to the conference organizers. When she saw the final publication, she noticed that somewhere between her submitting the bio and the bio going to print, someone had added a few lines about how much Nadiya cared about advancing diversity in the field. Obviously, having different perspectives in the mix was something Nadiya cared about. As a Tongan female in a largely White male industry, Nadiya cared about representation. But why hadn't the organizers consulted her before making that addition to her bio? There was no mention of diversity in any of the other speakers' bios. Why had the organizers put it in hers?

She hated being used as a token. She wanted to present herself in the way that she had chosen. Having words put in her mouth made her feel like she was a pawn. As much as was within her ability, she wanted to be sure she was seen as part of the lineup for the technical expertise she brought rather than just to break up the homogeneity of White male conference speakers. If they were going to add lines to her bio, the least they could do was consult her rather than make unilateral changes to how she was being presented. Adding and editing without her consent—even with an addition that she would agree with—detracted from her original voice.

Consent matters. Putting words in someone's mouth without their consent is a form of silencing. Edits are a normal part of working together, but consultation as to whether the changes resonate is a form of respect. Some might argue that agreeing to be part of the conference lineup gives organizers the license to frame the speaker as they wish. But we can do better to interrogate the impacts and biases as they manifest. The organizers could have consulted with

Nadiya, saying, "We'd like to add a few lines so attendees know they can ask questions, is that okay with you?" Having that exchange would have opened up the conversation about where the additions would be, why they were needed, and what impact they had on Nadiya.

Consent can also be tricky when telling our own stories inevitably implicates someone else's desire for privacy. Because our lives are inextricably tied to others' lives, it can be hard to figure out whether we can tell our story without sharing someone else's.

Jeong had been diagnosed with stage 4 cancer. He had no desire to share the diagnosis with anyone other than his wife. He didn't want his adult kids to worry about him. He didn't want to be a burden on anyone. He wanted people to remember him as the strong, healthy, adventure-loving person he had been prior to cancer. When family friends noticed he had lost weight, he attributed it to stress. When his hair started falling out, he stopped seeing friends. His friends assumed he was just busy, as Jeong and his wife, Anna, were in the process of downsizing their house. Anna knew him well enough to want to respect his privacy. She wanted to do whatever she could to make this season as tenable for him as possible.

At the same time, unable to tell anyone what was really going on, Anna began to feel untethered. Putting on a happy face and pretending everything was normal was draining. Never one to lie, she was out of reasons why she couldn't come for lunch or make time for a visit. She had turned from thriving socialite to weary caregiver. There were days she wanted to scream. Hot showers were her only solace; there she imagined the water would wash away the tears and cover her silent sobs. Jeong's desire for privacy silenced Anna.

One day when Anna hit a breaking point, she said, "Jeong, I know you don't want people to know, but I have to tell someone. I'm only going to tell my best friend and one neighbor so they can help support me." Voice and silence don't have to be all or nothing. Jeong can have the privacy that affords his dignity while Anna is able to receive the support she needs to keep on.

We silence people when we don't let them tell their version of the story. Implicitly or explicitly asking people to stay silent centers our needs over their own. There's no denying that sharing stories opens up the situation to all sorts of commentary, but whether we get to tell our story—our side of the story—shapes the world we live in and the weight we carry. Consider how your desire for silence impacts someone else's need for voice—and see if, like Anna, there's a way to honor both.

## We Rely on Flawed Reflexes

One of the choices I regret most in my professional life is an email I sent while walking home from the grocery store. It was a hot summer weekend. I checked my email and saw one from a colleague. Our team had been working on a job description for a new hire, in which we said we were an employer that valued diversity and inclusion. In reviewing the job description, my colleague inquired, "In what ways are we actually diverse and inclusive?"

My thumbs shot back a quick message. "I can think of at least 10 ways that we're diverse and inclusive. Will look forward to talking about it next week!"

I'm ashamed I didn't pause to inquire as to why she was asking, what she was concerned about, or to consider that even asking the question could feel like a big risk to her.

There are still times that I want to believe my reply wasn't all that off the mark. My colleague asked a question, and I provided an answer. I can justify my reply in so many different ways—that I was just channeling the existing culture and reinforcing the norms. That

I was embodying the enthusiasm expected of our team. That it wasn't actually *that* bad a response. My reply was consistent with the upbeat tone that leadership championed. I had suggested we move the topic off email and into real-time conversation. I hadn't meant to shut her down.

But the reality is that I did shut her down.

My reply failed to express curiosity as to the question behind her question. My quickness and brevity in reply further alienated her as a member of the team.

The measure of success in communication isn't what we mean, but what others take away. Success isn't our good intent, but what impact we have. And there I had failed.

All my explanations and justifications don't erase the fact that damage was done. My reply made her feel unheard, and that I wasn't open to what she might be trying to ask or say. She had taken the risk to speak up, and I hadn't worked to understand what she was really saying.

You might be thinking, *Well, you answered the question she asked. Why is it up to us to ask her to say more? She's the one who didn't actually say what she meant.*

We're all going to miss each other in communication at some point. I want and need to own my contributions to the conversation and the impacts I have on others. Here, resisting the habit of firing off an immediate response and pausing to think about what deeper question she might be asking would have helped nurture the culture of open conversation I want to build.

I share this example with the hope that it prevents you from silencing others with replies you haven't thought twice about. The culture of immediacy created by technological hyperconnectivity puts us all at risk for low-quality interactions and reactive decision making. I'm hoping you're less conditioned than I am, as I scan email on my phone while stopped at red lights and while walking home from the train station. I fire back replies in the forty-two seconds before jumping into the next meeting. I'm unfortunately one of the typical Americans that picks up their phone more than eighty times a day, which translates to an average of twenty-six hundred swipes, taps, and clicks a day.[8] Constant connection to the devices on our wrists, in our pockets, and at our fingertips has created an expectation that we will always be on and will provide and expect immediate replies. To cope with the expectation, our brains rely on reactive rather than reflective decision making.

Reflective decision making is logical, analytical, deliberate, and methodical. Reactive decision making is quick, impulsive, and intuitive.[9] We typically use reflective decision making to figure out significant questions, like whether to accept a new job, move to a new city, or continue being in relationship with someone. Reactive decision making isn't bad; it's an evolutionary adaptation that allows us to avoid the decision fatigue that results from continuous decision making. The problem isn't just that we're making bad decisions, it's that we often aren't even aware that there are decisions to make.[10]

Our brains leave it to our unconscious to make the vast majority of choices about our behavior. Only fifty of the ten million bits—or 0.0005 percent—of information our brains process each second is devoted to deliberate thought.[11] Going into autopilot allows us to perform tasks without thinking much about them.[12] Autopilot has its place. We don't typically need to think consciously about which way to tie our shoes or brush our teeth. We wouldn't function as seamlessly if we had to consciously deliberate every action. Our conscious minds build up databases to filter our real-time interactions. But the challenge is that our databases are colored by our unconscious biases and trigger reflexive habits. When we don't stop to pause, think, and choose a reply, the biases baked into our databases drive us.

Staying on autopilot means we perpetuate the existing norms of who has voice and who is silenced, including the norms baked into our own replies. We can improve our reflexive decision making by slowing down and making conscious choices in our replies.[13] We can stop doing what we've been conditioned to do and choose a different way.

## We Focus on Ourselves

Whether humans are inherently self-centered is a long-standing debate among philosophers and anthropologists. Whatever the theory, we need only look at the person next to us (or at ourselves) to know that humans gravitate toward what serves our wiring, preferences, and developed defaults. Researchers at the Duke Institute for Brain Science have found that humans can't help but prioritize stimuli that are associated with ourselves. Our brains literally respond faster when we hear our own name than someone else's.[14] If someone starts talking about me in a meeting, I'm far more likely to tune in to the conversation. We naturally focus on and prioritize what's good for ourselves.

Working and engaging in ways that play to our strengths requires less cognitive and emotional energy. The converse is true as well: working and engaging in ways that don't play to our strengths requires more energy. We silence others when we stick to our own defaults rather than choosing timing, mediums, and processing styles that support their voice.

## Time of day

Sabrina hated happy hours. There was the fact that she didn't drink and that team bonding was supposed to take place in loud bars where you could never hear anyone. But the biggest pain point was just the time of day. Scheduled for 5:00 to 6:00 p.m. on Thursdays, happy "hour" would run until 7:30, at which point the diehard crew would move to a local restaurant to continue the team bonding. No one seemed to understand that having work commitments outside of business hours wreaked havoc on her home life. Even if she could find someone to pick up the kids and get them to bed, the kids would act out for days after. One happy hour meant a multiday family hangover.

Yet those happy hours were where all the relationship building and informal brokering happened. It was over multiple scotches (or in Sabrina's case, tonic water with lime that looked like a gin and tonic) that you could catch wind of the changes that were coming down the pipeline and figure out whose favor you had to curry to stay in the running for the next prime project.

In a world that requires collaboration across time zones, figuring out a time to meet can feel like the hardest nut to crack. There is no getting around the reality that 9:00 a.m. in New York is 6:30 p.m. in Bangalore, 9:00 p.m. in Beijing, and 11:00 p.m. in Sydney. In a global world, there's no perfect hour. Employees in satellite offices have long taken calls outside local business hours under the supposed privilege of working for a multinational company with headquarters in a different country. Having different individuals flex working hours is one way to ensure that it's not always the same person "taking the hit."

But let's stop pretending that all time is created equal. The time at which events are scheduled limits who can be present, what costs people incur to be there, and whether the context plays to their strengths. The time of day we choose to meet silences or supports different people—based on who can make the meeting without messing up a semblance of a sleep schedule, or who is going to be firing on more cylinders at that time of day. Even if an individual is in attendance, the chosen time can silence or dull their contribution.

Author Carey Nieuwhof notes that everyone has green, yellow, and red energy zones of their day. Green zones are where you can focus best and are most productive. Yellow zones are when you can accomplish things, but not your greatest things. Red zones are when you're tired and have difficulty concentrating. Nieuwhof shares the example of the team meeting that was scheduled for 1:00 p.m. local time—which turned out to be in every attendee's red zone. Moving the meeting to a different time resulted in far more productivity, connectivity, and collaboration.[15] Meeting during someone's green zone supports their voice. Meeting during someone's red zone increases the likelihood that they are silenced or will choose silence.

I've been on calls—video off—while breastfeeding in the middle of the night because that is the only time people in a different time zone could meet. Some of those choices are the cost of doing business globally. Know that if you're going to schedule the meeting for 4:00 a.m. or 11:00 p.m. my time, you're not going to be getting my finest. That outcome may be the best of the options possible, but let's not pretend that it best supports my—or other peoples'—voice.

There may not be a perfect time that is green or even yellow for everyone—especially with multiple people across just as many time zones—but there are better and worse times. For example, there's never really a great time to tell someone that their work product is horrible or that you are breaking up with them. But there's a reason layoffs tend to happen on Fridays, and you don't tend to end a relationship on the other person's birthday.

In our internalized culture of immediacy, I may want to resolve issues as quickly as possible. Very few of us want to sit in the muck. We want to get out of the swirl and feel better about ourselves. We don't want people to think that we've been stewing on something. And there is a benefit to addressing issues before too much time has passed and our memories fail us. If we put off the conversation, we also run the risk of life crowding out the issue and never revisiting it. At the same time, we should consider whether it is a decent time for the other person as well.

As I write this, I have my toddler's refrain in my head—"But I want it right *now*!" How often do we act to satiate ourselves right now? I'm not talking about putting off the conversation for two weeks. But could we wait—and would the conversation and relationship benefit from waiting—twenty minutes? Just because you're ready to listen doesn't mean the other person is ready to talk. Ideally, you can jointly decide when to address a topic or pick up a conversation. Unilaterally deciding when typically means you're picking a time that works for you and that inclines the other person toward silence, even before the conversation has started.

## Communication mediums

Rabiyah loved large groups of people. For her, there was nothing as energizing as seeing people come together around a common interest. Loud music, flashy lights, and having to talk at the top of your lungs were the norm at a Rabiyah event. As her friends moved to different parts of the world, she tried to maintain the connection with annual gatherings and monthly video chats. But it wasn't the same.

She found typing cumbersome. Her eyes hurt having to stare at a screen for too long. The internet connection always lagged. She understood that group chats helped them stay connected, but she hated having to click through threads and not knowing when she was going to get a reply. At least if you had the person on the phone you knew what their response was right away.

In contrast, her brother, Omar, hated large family gatherings. He understood that family was important and that getting together was part of maintaining connection, but really, all the talking, music, and noise was overwhelming. Sensory overload, the textbooks called it. He was relieved when Rabiyah moved away and the choice was no longer between showing up at her parties (where he didn't actually get to talk with her) or being seen as a bad brother. Gone were the days when he'd need multiple days to recover from showing up to support Rabiyah. Reading a group email and replying when he was in the right frame of mind was far easier than having all the aunties talking at him all at once. Click an emoji button rather than figure out the right words to convey an emotion? That he could do. His family had always criticized him for hiding behind his phone, but really, it was easier for him to gather his thoughts, type them out, and read them again before clicking send instead of getting flustered in the moment.

Communication is a skill and an art—and each medium of communication requires its own skill and art. Being able to communicate asynchronously and in text-based formats requires different skill sets from being able to talk by phone, video, or in person. Each medium has its utility, and the combination allows us to stay connected, build relationships, and work together.

We tend to choose the mediums familiar to us and that play to our strengths. That can be difficult for anyone who doesn't share those strengths. Those who tout their ability to read people prefer to be in person, and certainly the mirror neurons in our brains that support empathy and relationship building are more active in person.[16] Yet being in person silences those who cannot travel or be physically present. Text-based communication has been criticized for its limited ability to communicate tone, but it also affords people time to think, the opportunity to craft messages, and documentation for those of us who outsource our memories to our inboxes or are concerned about legal liability.

We need to match the medium to the purpose of the communication and notice whose voice it amplifies and whose it silences. We do this by understanding how we're wired, which mediums make it easier or harder for us to use our voices, and how those same mediums support or silence the people around us. Choosing to meet in person prioritizes Radiyah's voice and has the potential to silence Omar. It's not to say that each of them shouldn't grow in the other skill set, but that we need to factor the impact of the medium when choosing a form of communication.

## Processing styles

Annette is a big personality and an external processor. She thinks best by talking through things in real time. Everyone knows everything about Annette, because "being in your face" is her brand. Her superpower is seeing an issue from all angles, so problems often get broader and larger in scope after talking to her. The upside? She sees the big picture. The downside? She sucks up all the space in the room.

Kai is the opposite. Deeply introspective and thoughtful, Kai processes best when uninterrupted. Give Kai a complex problem and two hours of quiet time and you'll get a fully formed analysis alongside a plan of nuanced action. Put Kai on the spot and expect an immediate verbal response, and Kai shuts down. Kai is a post-processor, where his best thinking will come after the meeting.

Kai is also mindful of creating space for his colleagues, to honor their preferences and desires. So when Annette goes on, he doesn't stop her.

Put Kai and Annette together, and it's a recipe for disaster. The more Annette talks—and she does—the more Kai withdraws. The more Kai withdraws, leaving a conversational vacuum, the more Annette fills the space. If this were reality TV, the rest of the team would watch with fascination and get second helpings of popcorn. But because this is real life, everybody cringes instead, knowing that they are all wasting hour after hour in meetings.

In the case of Annette and Kai, their respective wiring and preferences create a self-perpetuating cycle that amplifies Annette's voice while diminishing Kai's. One might think this dynamic works in Annette's favor, but being known as the one who is always talking and "sucking the energy out of the room" has done her no favors. Thinking *Here she goes again* means that people tune her out. Despite everyone's intention to be inclusive and collaborative team members, the entire team finds itself in an unproductive cycle.

Asking what processing style is best is an unfruitful question. Diversity extends to how our brains work. Neurodiversity is the acknowledgment that there are different ways people process the world around them. Given how different people are, it's no surprise that people's brains would also think, behave, learn, and feel in different ways.

The key question is how we can create relationships, teams, and organizations where different people can thrive. It is a challenge and opportunity to design communication patterns that leverage each person's strengths and mitigate the weaknesses. Such a pattern could be a meeting where questions are sent out ahead of time, so Kai can process them internally. In the meeting, Annette can help others make meaning about her actions by saying "I'm just thinking aloud" and be explicit in saying "Here's where I'm landing," so people know she's arrived at the destination after a potentially long and windy journey.

## We Change the Topic to Ourselves

For as long as he could remember, caring for his mother had been the primary focus of Dan's life. Now eighty-seven years old, her pacemaker was keeping her alive. She was on and off oxygen. His days were spent coordinating specialists, fighting with insurance companies, and managing the pain she felt. The nurses who came to provide in-home assistance called his mom "the cat with nine lives," because whatever the complication, she always made it through. Dan didn't resent taking care of her. After all, she was his mother.

Dan was the youngest of three siblings. His brother died in a car accident years ago. Nina was the middle child—the diva and mom's favorite. Nina had always dreamed of traveling the world. When she saved up enough for a plane ticket, she left. There would be months when no one in the family heard from her. When she reappeared, she'd be full of stories—how she'd climbed snowcapped mountains, tried whimsical food, and swum with sharks.

Mom had named Dan power of attorney, giving him authority to make her medical decisions. Her second stroke in nine months caused irreversible brain damage. After two weeks of therapies and the ventilator, Mom still showed no signs of improvement. The doctors kept talking about end of life. Dan wrestled with what to do. Was he willing to pull the plug because he wanted to be free? Or because getting to rest was what Mom would have wanted? As absent and independent as Nina had been, he also knew that having Mom alive provided Nina stability—even if she wasn't around. But in this state, it wasn't like Mom was really alive.

Dan tried to get ahold of Nina, but as always, the texts and emails went unreturned. An automated recording told him that her voice mail was full.

When Nina finally called him back, Dan told her of the decision. "It's time to let Mom go," he said.

"Are you kidding me? How can you take my mom away from me?" Nina replied.

Dan froze. Nina's response felt unfair to Dan. He had reoriented his life. He had put relationships on hold. He had done the work to make sure things were taken care of. There had been years where Nina could have spent time with Mom if that is what really mattered. Why did everything always have to be about her?

We silence others when we focus on our own reactions rather than on the other person and the heart of what they are trying to communicate. There is no doubt our own reactions are part of the puzzle and contain important information. And focusing on our own reaction in the moment has the effect of disregarding what the other person is trying to communicate. Changing the topic to our own reaction creates work for someone—not typically us, as we're too focused on ourselves—to return to the original topic, if ever.

When we make things about ourselves, we silence other people.

Dan had been trying to tell Nina that Mom's time had come to an end. The decision had been excruciating for him. He had been conflicted and knew how hard it would be for her to hear the news. He wanted her to know that after everything he and the medical team had done, letting Mom go was the decision he was going to make. But none of those thoughts made it into the conversation because Nina changed the topic to her own reaction.

When we're hurt, our tendency is to focus on ourselves—our own reactions, how we've been wronged, how deeply the situation cuts *us*. We forget that what the other person was raising was the original topic of conversation. My colleagues Douglas Stone and Sheila Heen call this dynamic *switchtracking*, as if the conversation has switched tracks on a train track.[17] To support rather than silence people, we need to stop changing the topic to ourselves. In the moment, we need to focus on what the person is trying to communicate rather than our reactions to what we think they are saying. We need to work to understand where they are coming from and what they are looking for from us.

## We Don't Believe Them

Yael and Nicolas were assigned to a client project. Nicolas was a veteran in the field; Yael was an up-and-comer. In the client meeting, Nicolas joked that women can't possibly be trusted to make policy decisions. After all, he quipped, women are far too emotional. Others in the room chuckled. Yael's eyes widened. Had Nicolas really just said that? He'd moved on quickly, and his charm belied the gravity of the statement he'd just made. No one else seemed to have noticed. Who was she to contradict the veteran? It was almost easier for Yael to believe that she had misheard him. But even if the client didn't take issue with the comment, she did. After all, every joke contains a grain of truth.

Yael wrestled with what to do. She hated having to tolerate jokes like that and didn't want to be part of a team that would let that sort of comment go. She wasn't comfortable raising the issue with Nico-las, as he could tank her career before it even started.

When she told the project manager about Nicolas's comment, the manager's reply confirmed the fears Yael already had about whether she would be taken seriously.

"Are you sure you heard correctly? It's one of your first client meetings and English isn't your native language. Maybe your nerves got in the way of your hearing."

The project manager did circle back after a few days with a note— "The client said you and Nicolas were both great. No complaints about either of you."

Yael sighed. What would it take for someone to believe her, much less do something about Nicolas's behavior? Even if the client didn't take issue with the comment, she did. Why didn't her opinion (and dignity) matter?

How we show up when someone takes the risk to speak up tells them whether to shut up. In a world of hearsay, it makes sense that a project manager who wasn't present in the meeting might be curious about what happened in the meeting. But the manager's defaults re-veal the biases ingrained in so many of us—to trust the expert, the veteran, the man. When our experiences are met with doubt, it makes us question ourselves.

Yael got the message. Don't bother me with these sorts of issues. Your perspective won't be taken as seriously as Nicolas's. As long as the client is happy, it doesn't really matter what happened in the meeting.

From harassment to pay inequity to what happened during after-school care, we need to start with a default stance of believing peo-ple with subordinated identities in order to support voice. Unequivocal support of the person who claims to be harmed may go against the "innocent until proven guilty" approach of modern judicial systems, but it is necessary to encourage voice. Assuming that people who raise issues are themselves guilty, particularly when they don't have the protection of a dominant identity, disincentivizes people from speaking up. Failing to believe that people who raise issues are telling the truth puts an additional burden of proof on the person and increases the likelihood people stay silent.

## We Hold a Fixed Mindset

As with many families, at large gatherings with my relatives, there was often a kids' table. It started out as a practical arrangement: there weren't enough seats at the dining table, the kids talked about different things than adults, kids could all fit at the rickety folding table rather than the rosewood adult table with real chairs, kids could make their own mess, and the adults could actually have a less interrupted conversation. As we all grew, the question became when does one graduate from the kids' table? How do we stop being seen as kids?

We silence others when we refuse to update our mental model of them. It is as if they're starring in a TV series and the character descriptions are written in stone. But even in a TV series, for the series to be renewed, the characters would have to evolve.

We hold static mental models of people for good reason. Doing so helps us streamline decision making, tune out the noise, and stay sane. We have a general sense of what to expect from people and figure out how we might interact (or not interact) with them. For relationships like the ones with the family members we see once a year and don't know quite how we're related, it may make sense to keep the character sketches static, to keep the kids as kids. But for people we interact with daily by choice or circumstance, the static character script is stifling. After all, I can only grow as much as your character description of me is allowed to morph.

At some level, it is easier to maintain a fixed mindset about who other people are and what role they play in our lives. Keeping your character description set means I don't have to open myself up to the possibility that you might burn me again or hurt me in the process of your growth. At the same time, refusing to be open to the possibility that you might evolve means I am effectively stuck with the last version of you I knew, and I've silenced all future versions of you that might emerge.

## We Build Cultures of Silence

One of my friends likes to remind me: I'm watching you.

If I brush off the Big Brother aspect of the comment, the refrain is a good reminder that my words and actions shape the culture of the team I'm on, the organizations I'm part of, and the family I love. My actions can either support or silence the people around me. Others are watching—to see whether and how we talk about issues. Whether and how we address inequity. Whether the way we live and the things we do actually support our claims that we value dignity, belonging, and justice for each and every human.

A nonprofit organization engaged my team to help them build skills around having difficult conversations. In diagnostic interviews with individuals on the team, I probed to better understand the challenge. What was it that made the conversations difficult?

People replied, We just don't talk about things here. It's like "not talking about it" is in the water.

Few people on the team could pinpoint where the silence was

coming from. They all just knew that it was there. Everyone had learned not to express disagreement or difference, to keep opinions to themselves, and to work around instead of with others. Silence had become an invisible force within the culture.

The good news is that culture arises from repeated behaviors that form norms. If we remain on autopilot, we will continue to perpetuate the silence we've learned and the ways we silence others. With greater awareness and intentional choice, however, we can support others' voices, even when they are different from our own.

Each of our words and actions has the power to sustain or disrupt the cultures on our teams, in our organizations, and in our families. Each of our words and actions has the power to support or silence others. What will we choose?

## We All Silence Others— But We Don't Have To

If at any point in reading this chapter you had a twinge of guilt or an oh-shit moment, I hope you take that as an invitation to increase awareness, reflect, and make intentional choices going forward. If you notice yourself getting defensive or saying "That's not me!" or "That's not what I meant," revisit those moments. Ask yourself what you could have done differently to support someone else's voice.

Remember, you're reading this because you want to do better—or your organization wants everyone to do better. In the past five chapters, I hope I have made you aware of how you have both been silenced and may have silenced others.

Now, in order to move forward, we need to collectively take a breath.

(I'll wait.)

It's time to move through the guilt and shame of what we may have done and into intentional action. Will our choices always be perfect? No. But continuing to learn and having the courage to try is far better than inaction. Starting in the next chapter, I'll share how you can shift into action.

# REFLECTION QUESTIONS

---

Which of the ways of silencing people resonated with you? Which didn't?

What are your default preferences for:

> What time of day to communicate?

> What medium to use?

> How are you best able to process information?

What changes might you consider so you don't unintentionally silence the people around you?

# Part II

---

# ACTION

# 6

# Find Your Voice

don't watch much television, but the one television show I've watched regularly over the years is *Top Chef.* The contestants are all accomplished—touting the awards they've received, the renowned chefs they've worked for, the Michelin star restaurants they've been part of.

But to win, the contestants can't just rely on their credentials. From cooking on open flame to creating dishes featuring local ingredients, each challenge requires the contestants to create dishes that are uniquely their own.

Episode after episode, contestants fall into the same trap. Chefs who don't typically cook fine dining will pull out tweezers to try to make their dish more elevated. Other chefs use sodium alginate to attempt molecular gastronomy, even though their normal style is unadulterated farm-to-table.

After tasting one of these creations, the judges express their disgust and frustration. Time and again, the judges chide the chefs.

"Just cook your own food!"

For many of the chefs, figuring out their own food is an existential struggle. Is your own food the food you grew up eating? Based on the technique you learned in culinary training? The food of the last restaurant you worked at? If you've spent your entire career producing dishes and replicating menus that others crafted, literally cooking someone else's food, how would you know what your own food is?

Similarly, if we've spent a lifetime channeling others' voices and executing on their vision for our lives, how would we know what our own voice is?

In this chapter, we'll shift from awareness to action, so that in the rest of the book we can focus on how to use our voices to shape the lives and world we desire. I'll share four components we can use to find our voices. Each component is necessary, and as with any change, the process is nonlinear. As you read the following, consider which part of the process you're currently in, and how you can use these components to structure your own journey of finding—or rediscovering—your voice.

## Cultivate Awareness

Years ago, a mentor said, "Elaine, I like your voice. Your voice is strong." At that moment, tears ran down my cheeks. Thirtysomething years into living on this earth and it was the first time someone outside of myself acknowledged that I had a voice. And by voice, you now know I don't just mean the timbre of the sounds coming out of my mouth—which, I've been told, for better or worse, are so soothing that I could have a backup career narrating sleep stories and meditations.

By voice, he meant having my own thoughts, opinions, and preferences—and having them matter. As I shared in earlier chapters, all the subconscious messages I've received over the years told me my voice didn't matter. Or my voice only mattered if it was doing someone else's bidding. That being quiet and staying silent were what would get me through. I'm female. I'm young. I'm an immigrant. I'm the only fill-in-the-blank identity in a room full of people who don't share those identities. I'm not supposed to take up space. I'm not supposed to be heard.

Or so I had come to believe.

And I know I'm not the only one.

If you're wondering where the defiant, declaratory voice you had when you came out of the womb went, fear not—it's still there.

Below are three truths to hang on to as you rediscover and refine your voice. I name these truths so that when you experience them in action, you'll know that you're on track.

## Your voice is worthy and deserves to be heard

You might be fighting me about this statement, and that's a good thing.

No matter what people have told you or how much they have put you down, each of us has thoughts and feelings of our own. We all have unique ways of moving through the world. And we all have needs, ideas, dreams, passions, worries—and the unique combination of all those things—that are unique to us.

I used to think that I was easily replaceable and interchangeable.

After all, if what work needed was a token Asian, there were several billion of us in the world to choose from. If what the law firm needed was a woman on their all-male team, half the global population fits the bill. If what my neighborhood needed was a friendly person, well, anyone can be that, right?

But what I realized is that I'm the only one who can be me.

No matter how similar we are, no matter how many characteristics, experiences, or values we share, no one can replace each of us and our voice in the world. We see and react to the world differently because of our lived experiences and wiring. We make different connections between ideas and people and things because of who we are. The world is less vibrant, less colorful, less creative without each of our unique thought patterns and expressions.

Sure, I bring the perspective of being an Asian American woman to my workplace. But how many other people in the world have the experience of facilitating learning development experiences across industries on six continents, and are able to hold space across culture, difference, and hierarchy?

How many other people wished for world peace when they blew out the candles on their fifth birthday, and still carry that wish as they move through the world?

Reducing myself to having worth or value based on only one of my identities diminished the reality that no one else in the world can be me.

Similarly, no one else in the world can be you.

The systems we are part of may not always give us a voice, but it doesn't deny the truth that we each do have one. If our voice is our thoughts, feelings, passions, cares, experiences, and what we choose to do with them, only you can be you. Don't deprive others of all you have to offer. Don't deprive yourself of the freedom to live as authentically as you desire.

Your voice might be dormant. It might have gotten weaker from disuse and feel like it has atrophied, hidden beneath layers of expectation, propriety, and responsibility. But it's there, and we'll find it. Because your voice, thoughts, and way of influencing the world are unique. And it matters.

## People are going to try to shape your voice

"You need more executive presence."

"Are you really going to wear that to the event?"

"There's no way you could possibly believe that."

"We really need someone to organize the potluck, and you would be perfect for it!"

From our bosses, coworkers, friends, and family to the robocallers that keep dialing your number, we all face outside forces vying to influence our thoughts, actions, and where we spend our time and talents. Whether it's telling you what you should be wearing or how you should show up in the team meeting, those people are using their voices. As they should.

Feedback is everywhere. But we don't have to take all feedback. Someone else's voice can be input into our own process, but it does not have to determine what we do or say. Our work is to sift through the input to figure out what we want to let influence us, in what measure, and to what effect—if any.

If she was honest, Yesenia was confused, overwhelmed, and bone-numbingly tired. Everyone was trying to pull her in every direction. They wanted her money, her time, her energy, and her life. Her friend had been trying to recruit her to join a women's advocacy group. "C'mon, Yesenia! You can't do it alone. You're hitting the glass ceiling and trying to play nice isn't going to get you to the next level." Her neighbor was trying to organize a community watch and told her that if she wasn't for the community, then she was part of the problem. She got the message from her church group that if she wasn't showing up to Bible study and serving on the worship team and wearing a smile as a greeter at the door, then she wasn't a good

Christian. In response, Yesenia would say that she would think about it or pretend that she had to check her schedule.

But inside? She wanted to scream at everyone in her life to just shut up.

When we begin to use our voice, people will try to dictate where and when and how. But none of us can do it all. You and your voice don't just exist to do others' bidding. Instead, you get to decide where and when you want to put the time, energy, and effort of sharing your thoughts, advocating for change, or supporting others. From climate change to human trafficking, from next quarter's priorities to whether to have a silent auction at the next school fundraiser, there are more than enough causes you could lend your voice to.

Ultimately, where you lend your voice will define your voice.

## Judgment—of your voice and who you are—is normal

Known for his practicality and strong work ethic, Joe's dad ran a handyman service. From as early as Joe could remember, he'd go along to different jobs with his dad. From patching holes in walls to laying tile to fixing plumbing, he could do it all. His dad had built a healthy client following and word-of-mouth referrals were endless.

The plan had always been for Joe to take over the business. He went to a local college to study business administration, supposedly so that he could learn how to run the family business better. But while Joe didn't mind working with his dad when he was a kid, the work didn't come naturally to him. His father loved to tinker; Joe didn't. What Joe loved was art. He knew his parents didn't think art was practical, but alone with a palette, canvas, and brush was when Joe felt most whole.

How was art going to mesh with his family's plans for him to take over the handyman business? There was nothing wrong with being a handyman. The work was practical, it paid the bills. Joe's desire to do something different wasn't a knock against his dad, but an acknowledgment of his own gifts and skills.

As his dad spoke excitedly about how Joe would be able to take the business to the next level, Joe remained quiet. "What's going on, Joe?" asked his dad.

"I want to be a painter, not a handyman," Joe shared.

"How are you going to make a living painting? You can paint walls on projects. You want everything I've built to go to waste?"

"Fixing things is your dream, not mine," replied Joe.

"This wasn't my dream. Life isn't about dreams," said his dad. "We do what we need to do to provide for our families. And now it's your turn. Painting art is a hobby, not a job."

How could Joe let the family business die? How could he disrespect his father after all his dad had done for their family?

But handyman work was his father's work, not his. Art was the one thing that made him feel alive. He would regret it if he never gave art a real shot.

Like Joe, we all experience the judgment of others and the judgment we have about ourselves and the choices we make. We silence our own desires and voices because of others' judgments, or what we think will be their judgments. But whatever choices we make, judgment will exist.

Sifting through others' voices is especially difficult when the opinions come from those we care about. When you hear the judgment creeping in, acknowledge that others get to have their opinion. Then decide how much weight you want to give their input. Finding our voice is fundamentally about being okay with who we are and what we value, and continuing to make the choices that we can live with, regardless of what others think.

# Interrogate Our Voices

Once we are aware that we have a voice, and that people's attempts to influence and judge our voice is not reason to think we don't have one, we can start to figure out what aspects of our voice we want to keep and which we want to reexamine. Regularly interrogating your voice by challenging your own thinking and giving yourself permission to show up as you intend acknowledges the reality that we are ever-evolving human beings who are constantly learning.

## Challenge your own thinking

Kerri was living her dream. Her home was an idyllic cottage with crisp white fencing and a fresh green lawn. As a child, Kerri had been homeschooled. Her mom stayed at home, and Kerri appreciated growing up that way. Now, she was raising her kids in the same way. They could play safely in the cul-de-sac, and often did with their twelve-year-old neighbor Maya. Maya's parents both worked and traveled a lot, so Kerri was glad she could help out her neighbors by keeping an extra eye out for Maya.

Kerri was raised in a conservative Christian family, and some of her earliest memories were marching in pro-life protests. Her parents had always instilled in her that she needed to love her neighbors, and that her neighbors included people she couldn't see. She was proud to be able to speak for babies who couldn't speak for themselves. A speaker at a protest had introduced the toddler test—

if it wouldn't be okay to do something to a toddler, why would you do it to a baby in utero? That test stuck with her, and she continued to join the protests each year.

One day, there was a knock on her door. Kerri was surprised to find Maya on the front porch. "Can I come in?" asked Maya, her chin wobbling.

"Sure. The girls are at soccer, but you're welcome to stay."

At first Maya didn't say much. She nibbled on the cheese and crackers that Kerri offered her.

"Can I tell you something?" Maya asked timidly.

Kerri felt rage and confusion in her body and hot tears on her cheeks as Maya told her that her dad had raped her. And that Maya was now worried that she was pregnant. She had biked to the drugstore on her own and stolen a pregnancy test because she didn't want anyone to see her buying a test. The test was positive. Maya didn't know what to do.

"You're the only one I can talk to. And please don't tell my parents. They fight enough already, and I can't make things worse," finished Maya.

For many nights after that conversation, Kerri couldn't sleep. Her heart broke for Maya. She wept for the loss of innocence, the dysfunction, the trauma, and the childhood that would never be.

Kerri thought about her own daughters, the same age as Maya. Could they really carry a baby to term? Could they be expected to carry a child inside them who was a reminder of how their dad wasn't the dad he was supposed to be? She flashed back to all the marches she had been part of. The toddler test hadn't covered this situation. Kerri had spent all those years marching and fighting for life. Could she drive Maya to the clinic to end a baby's life? Kerri wanted to be a light in the darkness. What did that mean here?

Our beliefs don't exist in a vacuum. Our values are expressed by the things we say and do. Real-life situations can force us to examine what our beliefs look like in practice, and if and how the beliefs and values might evolve. We have to ask ourselves, Do I actually believe this—or have I simply never stopped to question it?

Actively ask yourself, What do I actually think? Regardless of others' opinions, what do I think? If I wasn't worried about consequences, what would I do? How would I explain my reasoning?

From there, ask yourself, What do I actually believe? Failing to challenge our own thinking means that we're living on autopilot, and complicit in perpetuating the defaults that others around us have set.

After interrogating our own thinking, we may come to the conclusion that what we thought we believed is actually what we still believe. Interrogation isn't about assuming an outcome or a change in a worldview. It's about standing on even more solid ground, having challenged ourselves in the process to articulate why we hold these beliefs. Interrogation is about making sure you are living in alignment with yourself and that your views are fully defensible to yourself.

This type of thinking can be disorientating, so much that many of us fear even asking *What do I really think?* in the first place. And rightfully so. Because being aware of what you really think and believe means you'll need to choose what to do next. If challenging your thinking causes you to diverge from the status quo, you might find yourself asking: How do I reconcile what I believe with what I've been taught? What does it mean for my relationships with people who believe something different? Is it disrespectful to my culture, parents, friends, family, religion, and community to believe differently? Then what?

You might also experience shame, wondering why you didn't interrogate your own thinking earlier. How could I have gone so long through life without questioning this belief? Or my actions and behaviors? What trail of damage have I left behind? How do I repair my relationships and move forward?

But tuning in to what you—not your boss, your friend, or your loved one—think is essential for knowing your own voice and living a more intentional, aligned life. And each of us finds our own voice in our own time.

In saying all of this, have I talked you out of doing this interrogation?

I hope not. Because this is the work of figuring out your voice, rather than simply holding on to the beliefs, practices, expectations, and responsibilities that you might have taken on from others over the years. Challenging your thinking doesn't have to be all day, every day, nor does it have to be an existential crisis. It is simply observing the world around you and the conversations you're in to say, Do I agree with this?

And if not, what do I actually think?

## Give yourself permission

The other day, someone I'd just met thanked me for giving her permission to be herself. It struck me that this person felt the need to get permission. After all, she is a wildly talented leader with a unique ability to balance clarity and compassion. She has built a product and community that I never could have imagined.

And yet, I could also see why she might be looking for permission to be herself. As an Arab woman leading in corporate America, she's navigating many of the same influences that made me conform and contort myself to the voices and styles I had seen around me for most of my career—and more. I was delighted that our interaction gave her permission to be herself.

At the same time, there was no reason why she needed me to give her permission to be herself. Too often we look to those around us—especially higher up on the org chart or family tree, or those we deem as having authority—to give us permission. It makes sense, as those people have influence over whether we're seen as doing a good job at work or honoring the family. In the absence of making the implicit explicit, it's easy to assume that we need other people to grant us permission. After all, we're used to having to ask for permission from others—to go to the restroom, stay out late, or take days off work. We are acculturated to ask for permission.

But who do we really need permission from? Often it's not permission from others, but from ourselves. Permission to be the version of ourselves we want to be and could be.

Are you waiting for permission from other people to have a voice? What would it look like for you to give yourself permission—to think for yourself, to do what you believe is good, right, and worthwhile, and to be wholly and unabashedly yourself?

Well-meaning people often say, "Don't ask for permission, ask for forgiveness." The essence of the message seems sound—take action, don't let others hold you back. At the same time, if forgiveness isn't granted as easily to people like us, the advice falls flat. Part of finding your voice is figuring out what level of risk, consequence, and uncertainty you are willing and able to take on.

The work of wrestling with what our voice is can be challenging—and worthwhile. Knowing what we believe, what we aspire to, and who we are seeking permission from only goes so far. To figure out whether a voice is really ours, we have to try behaviors on for size.

# Experiment with Using Your Voice

After interrogating our beliefs, we must turn those ideals into action. That in turn helps us cultivate our own voice. An easy way to practice this in everyday life is with experiments.

Doing an experiment always takes me back to middle school science. If you put baking soda and white vinegar in a two-gallon soda bottle, what happens? The focus of an experiment is curiosity and learning, not just results. You're trying something to see what happens, rather than being locked into an outcome. Experiments provide data that can inform our actions going forward.[1] For those of us who are outcome-oriented perfectionists, experiments prevent us from getting bogged down in inaction because we're worried about the outcome. Experimentation allows us to break free from the weight of having to achieve so we can learn from trying *something*.

So how do you get started?

## Do small experiments

Let me be clear, I'm not suggesting you stop reading now to go tell your boss why they suck. Instead, start with an experiment that allows you to take a calculated risk in a context where you know you can weather the consequences.

For me, a small experiment was asking whether a taxi driver could open the windows because it was stuffy in the cab. I know. That's how small I had to start because of how deep-rooted my learned silence was.

I had just landed in Seattle. After a few hours in airports and airplanes, I was craving some fresh air. It was a muggy day and there was nothing fresh about the air freshener that dangled from the rearview mirror. I pushed the button to open the passenger window, but the window didn't budge. I tried it again, just for good measure.

I thought:

*Don't bother the guy. The GPS says there's only twenty-two minutes left of the ride. You'll be fine. You can deal with the discomfort.*

You might also be making fun of me that such a simple request caused me so much angst. Was the driver going to get mad at me for asking? Was he the type who would take his annoyance out on me by driving recklessly? I was a female traveling alone in a city I wasn't familiar with.

At the same time, we were on a major freeway, so the chances of me ending up in a ditch for asking the guy to open the window were pretty low.

I talked myself into it.

*Asking to open a window is a pretty reasonable request. The worst case is that he says no. You'll never see the guy again.*

"Sir, would you mind opening the window? It's a little stuffy in here," I said.

Without a word, he pushed a button. The window opened.

The air was glorious—fresh and crisp, tasting of freedom and validation.

Asking the cab driver to open the window was a successful experiment. Not because he acted upon my request, though that was a nice perk, but because I learned something in that moment. I learned that I can make a request of someone and the world won't end. I can ask for what I need, and I might even get what I ask for.

It seems laughable to me that as a grown woman I'd spend so much energy questioning whether I can make an ask of someone I've never met and will likely never encounter again. But this is the type of small experiment that, repeated over time, changes our understanding of whether we have a voice and what our voice looks like. The power to decide what experiments we take on also increases our tolerance for risk and willingness to wait for longer-term rewards.[2]

I expressed a point of view and made a request. I learned that asking won't kill me, and in fact, asking might lead to an outcome that better meets my needs. I'm unlearning what I've learned about denying my own needs in order not to impose on others. I'm unlearning the instinct to put up with things and learning to communicate what it is I need or want. I'm learning that there is validity to my own needs and that using my voice actually has impact.

## Make experiments time bound

Unsurprisingly, being able to return online purchases for free increases the likelihood that people make the purchase. One study showed that free returns boosted customer spending 357 percent, whereas having to pay for return shipping decreased spending with the retailer.[3] Knowing that we can return purchases with no financial cost makes it easier for people to decide to make the purchase.[4]

Similarly, trying experiments of voice on for size lowers the stakes for us to try *something*. If the behavior doesn't fit, you aren't stuck with it forever.

The trick is to try a behavior or stance for long enough to get some real data, but not long enough that a fear of commitment raises what you perceive as the stakes. Even if they feel like the longest days, we can do most anything for a few days. Choose a length of time no longer than thirty days for your next experiment. For example, for meetings in the next three weeks, I'm going to share my perspective. Or for the next three weeks, I'm going to set a clear boundary with my mother-in-law about whether she can comment about my weight. Or in my next three one-to-one meetings with my manager, I'm going to answer their questions candidly. Putting a time limit on the experiment lowers the stakes because you know it won't last forever. At the same time, you're able to gather information and then adapt based on what you learn.

## Get comfortable with being uncomfortable

Experimentation can feel awkward, understandably so because you're trying something new. As you change your behavior, others might have strong reactions as they figure out how to react to a different you. Others might also not notice any difference or have any reaction—after all, we tend to pay more attention to and judge ourselves more harshly than others judge us.[5] All these reactions are data—information for us to figure out what we're learning and how that informs our decisions about our voice in the future. As uncomfortable as a new behavior might feel, know that discomfort is part of experimentation, and that experiments are time bound.

So, what small experiment will you try? With whom? About what? Is it telling the barista that they messed up your order and you'd like to get what you actually ordered? Sharing with your co-worker the impact it had on you when they didn't invite you to the meeting? Communicating that you don't want to go to an event on Thursday night because there are already too many moving parts to your life?

What constitutes a small experiment will depend on where you're at with building your muscles for voice. But start somewhere with a calculated risk you can absorb. My hunch is that like me in the taxi, you'll find that you might get what you want. And you'll be one step closer to being known, getting what you need, and shaping the world to be one in which you want to live.

## Invite Voices into the Mix

Life isn't a solo sport. Our lives are too intertwined with others' lives and our environments for us not to impact each other. So whether or not we invite feedback, other people's opinions, judgments, and reactions are going to be coming our way. Which voices will we listen to? Which voices will we let have influence over us? This component of finding your voice is all about feedback.

### Balance the inputs

My best friend likes to tell me, "You do you."

At this point, it's a mantra that needs to be tattooed on my forehead, or at least emblazoned on a mug in my hand.

Yet every time she says it, I'm thinking, *But I can't just do me! I'm responsible for all these people—my family, the people I lead, and the community around me.*

But that mantra is one that I need in my ear, because it is a perspective I all too quickly forget. I'm prone—like many of us—to think about everyone else before myself. My friend knows my defaults and can offset my tendency to think about everyone but myself so I don't fall into the same well-worn traps. She knows what I aspire to and keeps pointing me in that direction—even as I get distracted.

Naysayers, mansplainers, and people with their own agenda will always exist. They have a way of making themselves known to us— even if we wish they wouldn't. Unfortunately, we don't always have the option to block them out. So we need to choose what weight we give them and ensure that those voices are not the only ones in our lives.

Do you have voices you trust to help you weather the waves of unsolicited opinion? Who are the voices you trust and admire who are going to counterbalance the negative inputs? Curate the mix to include people who have your best interests at heart, who are genuinely on your team, who are going to point out what is best for you—and hopefully in ways that make it easy for you to hear them. We need people who know us well enough to help us spot patterns, ask clarifying questions, and remind us who we are.

Who is currently in your ear and in your life? What voices might you need to invite in to make the journey more sustainable? Don't leave the inputs to chance. Intentionally curate the inputs that are going to nourish and support you.

## Have a sounding board

Gabe was stuck in a rut. He'd been in the same job for seven years, which was multiple lifetimes in the start-up world, where people typically change jobs at least every few years. As a well-connected White man in tech, he didn't doubt that he could land something else. The challenge was just knowing what he actually wanted to do. His mentors at work were telling him to go for the next promotion. His significant other wanted him to wait out the company's IPO to see if they could cash out and pay off the house. His brother wanted him to quit his job entirely so they could travel the world together. At night Gabe lay awake cycling through the options, none of which seemed like they'd be any better for him, even if they would make other people happy.

Spinning and spiraling in your own thoughts, only to get nowhere, is a waste of time and energy. And yet, 73 percent of adults between the ages of twenty-five and thirty-five overthink, as do 52 percent of people between the ages of forty-five and fifty-five.[6] Overthinking gives rise to more negative thoughts and freezes us from taking action. Dwelling on shortcomings, mistakes, and problems increases risk of mental health problems and interferes with solving problems.[7] Along with inviting in different inputs, inviting people to be sounding boards can help us sort out our voice from the others vying for influence in our lives.

"But Gabe, what do *you* want?" his colleague asked as they took their daily walk.

"I want everyone to get off my back so that I can figure out what I want. I want enough energy and space so I can actually think," Gabe replied, exasperated.

"Sounds like you know what you want. Make *that* happen."

Seeing ourselves accurately without the help of others is impossible. Parsing through the things we're stewing on with others can get us to clarity faster, in part because putting feelings into words reduces the activity in the emotionally reactive part of our brains.[8]

But note that the invitation is for someone to hold up a mirror and help you hear what you're saying, not to offer their own advice. The origin of the term *sounding board* comes from the device—often an actual board—positioned over a stage, podium, or pulpit that helps amplify the speaker's voice.[9] A sounding board is someone you can try out ideas with, *not* someone who is going to make things worse by cycling on even more negativity. While studies show that social support generally reduces stress and burnout, we all know that not all social support is the same. Excessive negative talk about an issue with someone else—called co-rumination—actually leads to increasing levels of stress and burnout.[10]

As you experiment with your own voice, test ideas and approaches with people you trust. The intent is not to let other people make the calls in your life, but to avoid spinning in the theoretical and get to practical action.

## Decide whose voices are essential

When my husband and I were planning our wedding, we made a list of people that had to be present when we made our vows. These were the people around whom we were willing to schedule our lives in order for them to be there. We knew that in navigating the many expectations of family and community, there would be far too many opinions and pulls. If we didn't make a list of essential people, we would forever be managing everyone's expectations.

After we agreed to the list and a date that everyone on the list could make, I discovered it was a date that a dear colleague of mine couldn't make. I felt the twang of disappointment, as I would have ideally loved for them to be there. But they weren't on the list. And we weren't going to upend all the other calibrating we had done to accommodate someone who wasn't on the list.

We're told that we have to be considerate of others and open to feedback. But hearing someone out doesn't mean that we have to take their advice or let their opinion drive our lives. Some of the voices have to become noise. At the end of the day, as receivers of feedback, we get to decide what we want to take on. We get to decide how much weight and power others' opinions have over us. We can listen and decide that their input is going to go in the discard pile—or at least the "doesn't have so much weight in my life" pile.

We do so by getting clear on whose voices we deem essential. You can get this clarity by answering the following questions for yourself:

Whose needs do I *have* to solve for here?

Who are the top three people or groups of people I need to consider and communicate to about this issue? (Make sure to include yourself as one of the stakeholders!)

Whose disappointment can I live with?

You can also use the three buckets tool from chapter 5 to sort your stakeholders. The voices of the people who *decide* with you are essential. The voices of those in the *consult* bucket are ones that you are inviting in, but can also choose not to listen to. The people in the *inform* bucket have no business adding noise to your calculation.

Whose opinion is essential will depend on the topic and context you're navigating. But having the awareness that you don't have to solve for everyone helps combat our tendency to try to take on the impossible task of making everyone happy. If they aren't on the list, they don't get to have power over you.

## Invite your own reflection

Finding your voice is about strengthening your own sense of self. What do you believe? How do you live in greater alignment with the values you hold? How do you move through this world and have the impact *you* want on your family, organizations, and community? While others' perspectives are valuable, our perspective is ultimately what determines our voice. Reflecting on our choices puts us in the driver's seat and reminds us that we are key stakeholders in our own lives. We have the agency and autonomy to evaluate what we've learned, what we appreciate, and what we didn't like about the experiments we tried.

We can create our own intentional feedback loop by answering the following questions for ourselves after each experiment:

What did I learn?

What do I want to try again?

What would I do differently?

## Regularly recalibrate

None of us are static human beings. We are each ever evolving. The constant evolution means we need to keep taking stock of whether our voice is becoming muted or dull, whether we've slipped into old habits or let others have more influence over us than we intend. When facing bigger life transitions, that might mean taking stock daily. When navigating business as usual, that might mean a quarterly pulse check with yourself or your sounding board.

Many of us worry about being perceived as inconsistent or going back on our word if we change. But finding your voice isn't a linear or once-and-done process. Instead, finding your voice is an ongoing exercise.

Life happens.

People change.

Priorities shift.

Different situations help clarify what our voice is, what we truly value, and who we are. It is through the pushing and pulling, nudging and tension that we figure out the contours of our voice. Finding your voice means figuring out what version of yourself you want to bring forward to the circumstances you face today, tomorrow, and in the days to come.

IN THIS CHAPTER WE'VE COVERED FOUR NONLINEAR COMPONENTS to finding your voice. We have built baseline *awareness* of the dynamics at play, and why losing your voice might even be an issue in the first place. As we *interrogate* our choices, *experiment* with new approaches, and *invite* others and ourselves into intentional reflection, your voice will become stronger and clearer—to yourself and those around you. The more time you spend with your own voice, the more familiar it will become. Knowing who you are and what you think brings you into alignment with yourself. If you have an increasing sense of your own voice, how do you use that voice to have the impact you want?

# YOUR TURN

---

## Awareness

- Do you believe you have a voice? Why or why not?

- What did you notice as you read the Awareness portion of the chapter?

## Interrogate

- As you listen to someone talk (this could be on the news, in a meeting, or in conversation between friends), ask yourself: Do I agree? What do *I* think about the topic? About how things are being handled? Notice where you agree or disagree with the majority opinion.

## Experiment

- What do you want to try?

- For how long will you run the experiment?

## Invite

- What kind of voices do you need to invite into the mix?

- Who could be a sounding board for you?

# 7

# Use Your Voice

New to the team, Leila knew she had to make a good impression.

But the weekly meetings—her main connection with the team—were shit shows.

Having thirty-five people on a call across time zones—with some people on video, some people off, some people in conference rooms with spotty audio connection, some people at home with kids running in the background—meant that half the meeting was spent repeating the same things.

The company's chief technical officer, Sharath—Leila's boss—didn't see the problem. He said, "Having everyone in the meeting helps us get on the same page." It was true. No one could pretend they didn't know what to do. But it was also true that people with less experience—like Leila—felt intimidated by speaking up in front of thirty-four colleagues.

In meeting after meeting, Leila couldn't get a word in. The well-worn cadence of the project team left no room for a newbie like her to add to the conversation. By the time she had formed her thought, the meeting had moved on. When she tried to assert herself, someone inevitably talked at the same time.

As the only person without a technical background on the team, Leila wanted to be sure that people could see that she still brought value. She watched as they spoke their minds, in seemingly effortless ways, and pined for the days when she didn't second-guess and overanalyze her every move.

The rare occasion when someone asked her what she thought, Leila froze. This was her moment. She had to say something. Something insightful. Something mind-blowing. Something that would show people why she belonged at the table. But inevitably she would choke. Her mind blank, she'd mutter sheepishly, "Looks like you've got it all covered." Once again, she had missed her shot. And beating herself up for hours afterward about it didn't help either.

In her first review, Leila got feedback from her manager that she needed to speak up and be more visible—for others to see what she was bringing to the team. It stung when someone asked her whether she was just there to take notes. She wasn't. She was making the whole project run. But after a lifetime of being snapped at and ripped apart by others, her instinct to defer to those in power ran deep. She hated talking over others, having to fight for airtime, and was irrationally annoyed by a meeting in which people had to repeat themselves four times to be heard because everyone was distracted and frustrated by the meeting itself.

Doing the work to find our voice is just the start. We also need to understand, practically, how to speak up.

In this chapter, I offer three levers to do just that. By using substance, relationship, and process as cheat codes, we can figure out how to use our voices in ways that are both additive to groups and authentic to ourselves.

## Three Levers for Voice

In the 1980s, my colleagues at the Harvard Negotiation Project noted that each negotiation is the confluence of three different dimensions: substance, relationship, and process. We are simultaneously negotiating the substance (what), the relationship (who), and the process (how). Failing to pay attention to any of these dimensions means that we're missing out on a key factor that can shape the outcome of the negotiation. The dimensions have long provided a framework for mediators to hold the space for difficult conversations by tending to the relationship and managing the process in a way that most individuals don't.

What I've discovered in figuring out how to use my own voice and coaching others to use theirs is that these dimensions also serve as levers for voice. Substance, process, and relationship can serve as a mental model for using our voices, especially when we question what we have to add. In short, if you don't see yourself as the expert on the topic of conversation (substance), you still have two more ways to impact the conversation. The levers provide a mental shortcut for thinking about where and how you join the conversation and are fundamentally able to shape the conversation. Below, I'll detail the relationship between the three levers and offer practical ways to use each lever to support your own voice.

## Substance

Substance is *what* we're talking about.

Whether discussing what we're going to have for dinner, revenue projections for the quarter, or the technical specifications of a project, the substance is what we typically think of as the topic of conversation. The most common reasons people give for not saying what they think about a topic include not being the subject matter expert, feeling underqualified, and not wanting to create conflict.

For years, Derrick's aunt had been telling him to purchase life insurance: "It will cover your family if the worst thing happens to you. The money you put in will grow tax-free." While the individual words and phrases made sense to him, looking at rows of numbers and projected values made Derrick's eyes glaze over. Talking about cash-value accumulation, non-guaranteed dividends, and probate-free legacy made his head spin. He wanted to be responsible for his family, but he didn't understand how paying a bunch of money up front made sense, especially given how much his income varied each year. He was never effective in debating his aunt, as she always had a comeback or chart for any of his questions. He remained hesitant to purchase any policy that he didn't fully understand.

While it makes sense that we might tread lightly on topics we don't consider our expertise, to dismiss or deny our perspective simply on those grounds means that we miss out on what we each bring when it comes to the substance. We each have perspective and insight to add, even if we don't see ourselves as the subject matter expert. If you're doubting whether you have standing to speak on the substance, you can zero in on what you might add by asking and answering two questions for yourself:

## What aspects of the substance are in my domain?

Even if Derrick isn't an expert in the ins and outs of life insurance policies or financial planning, he is an expert on his family's short- and long-term financial goals and comfort level with different institutions. While his aunt's domain is presenting options and advising out of good intentions, Derrick's domain is identifying what really matters to him and his family. Even if he doesn't feel like he can debate his aunt effectively on the merits of life insurance, he is the subject matter expert on his own reactions, bandwidth, comfort level, and, ultimately, his own decisions about where to put the money he has.

Whereas Leila's domain, as a project manager, is project scope, planning, cost, resourcing, and timeline. Her job is to identify the risks that may impact the project and take steps to reduce the risks. Even if the chief technology officer doesn't want to hear about the risks and dismisses them by saying, "Just make it happen," communicating the risks is Leila's job. It doesn't mean that she won't receive flack for pointing them out. But knowing that identifying risks is in her domain can remind her that she has a legitimate place at the table and reason to engage the conversation. Knowing your domain helps counter the doubts we can have as to whether we can rightfully add to the conversation, particularly when faced with strong personalities and people who seem very sure of their own expertise.

If it's not clear what your domain is from a job description or conversation about roles, those are conversations to have so you have more solid footing from which to speak. You can start by listing what you assume your role is and checking the description with the people you assume are the decision makers. Clarity allows you to stop wondering and spinning, and for others to answer questions that they might not know existed.

Whether at work or home, no one is more expert about ourselves and our needs and preferences than we are. Owning our preferences and needs as our domain—in addition to whatever strength we bring—helps us remember that there's substance that we can represent. We are the subject matter experts about ourselves and what we need.

## What perspective do I bring?

Many of us assume that if we're new to the team or more junior, we might have less to offer. And certainly others' behaviors toward us can reinforce those assumptions. But whether based on life experience, life stage, geographic location, tenure in the organization, or identity, each of us brings a different perspective to topics and the world. People who have been in a project or system for years have weak points. The longer you've been in a work or family system and gotten used to the way things are done, the less able you are to see what's problematic—and how you could improve things. We need fresh blood and fresh eyes to be able to see things clearly.

A key shift we can make is to move from the assumption that we have less to offer, to noting that we have something different to offer. We can own our unique lenses by naming the lens through which we're speaking, using phrases like the following to add our perspective to the mix:

"From where I sit . . ."

"Looking at it from an immigrant perspective . . ."

"As a digital native . . ."

"If I put my customer support hat on . . ."

"Coming to this project with fresh eyes . . ."

"As someone who has been married—and divorced . . ."

Ideally, we wouldn't need a qualifier in order to say what we think. But to the extent that we're wondering how to get a word in edgewise or question whether what we have to say adds value, nam-

ing the specific lens from which you're speaking can remind others
(and yourself) of what you bring. Identifying a specific vantage point
takes the pressure off and allows us to speak more objectively about
the issue from our own lens. It allows us to own the reality that we
each do see things differently and to recognize that different perspectives are valid, valuable, and legitimate. And it allows us to communicate about impacts and perceptions that others might not have
considered from where they sit.

## Relationship

If substance is the *what*, relationship is the *who*—who is involved,
how each person is feeling treated, the level of trust, and how people
are impacted by each other.

Chinyere and Jason were overwhelmed. Juggling two careers
while raising kids and caring for their aging parents was too much.
When the opportunity came up to move across the country so Jason
could take an executive role and be closer to family, they jumped at
it. Soon, the days became a blur. As high-performing individuals
skilled in project management, Jason and Chinyere assumed that if
anyone could pull this move off, they could. But as the weeks passed,
they moved more like ships passing in the night than the life partners they had set out to be.

Sure, the kids got to their classmate's birthday party with clothes
on their backs. There was food in the fridge, and their performance
reviews at work were positive. Working at night, they were able to
figure out the logistics of the move. But after a particularly fraught
day trying to line up caregivers in between investor meetings and
seeing Jason's latest text about why the dog was puking, Chinyere

responded, "You feel like a business partner rather than my life partner. Yes, we need to figure out the logistics and why the dog is sick again, but I'm worried that even after the move, after the kids are grown, there isn't going to be an us."

When Chinyere arrived home, frazzled and tired but ready for a fight, Jason pulled her in for a hug. "We'll figure it out," he said. "We'll make sure there's an us."

Sometimes, relationship is the heart of the matter. Relationship is whether we feel connected to or alienated by the people we care about, whether we feel respected and accepted, and whether the boundaries we have feel healthy. Relationship is core to having social capital, defined as the benefits one gets because of who you know,[1] that contributes to better overall organizational performance.[2] Relationship is what's implicated when someone turns off their camera during the video call so people can't see how enraged they are or how Engineering is going to react to the latest pivot. Relationship is all the people dynamics that are the pain point for most managers, the key reason people daydream of having a different family or friends.

To put a finer point on it, relationship is why 65 percent of start-ups fail because of cofounder conflict,[3] and about half of marriages globally end in divorce or separation.[4] And it makes sense—as we're focused on paying the bills, figuring out our taxes, making sure there's food on the table, trying to keep kids and pets alive and out of trouble, tending to someone's emotions, ego, and needs is often the last thing we want to do. Like Chinyere and Jason, when we focus on substance, we often fail to tend to relationship. But it also means that relationship is a powerful lever for voice.

In any aspect of our lives, tending to relationship by anticipating, understanding, and solving for how the people involved feel heads off additional complexity and builds toward the dignity we crave. We can add our voice by asking the following questions, out loud or to ourselves, to make observations: Who is left out? How are people feeling? Who is engaged? Who is disengaged? What is building or reducing trust? Who has been silent? Who might feel silenced? Tending to the human reactions and tendencies in any dynamic allows us to surface issues, air grievances, and problem solve sooner.

Paying attention to relationship also allows you to use your voice to disrupt bias and cultivate the emotional culture of your family, community, or company.

## Disrupt bias

Using your voice doesn't have to be about having the answer to a technical problem or knowing the cure for cancer. Being able to use your voice to tend to the relationship dynamics at play allows you to shape the world around you. Feelings are often misread by others. Focusing on relationship allows you to mitigate biased interpretations of emotions at work, where women and people of color are judged more harshly for expressing emotion than White men.[5]

"You need to be less aggressive. If you can't be more of a team player, we can't have you on the calls with the client." Zuri's blood boiled as she heard the older male partner offer her, in his words, constructive coaching.

She clenched her teeth and steadied her breath as she looked around the room. She knew that as a young Black woman in private equity, anything she said in the moment would be used against her.

"I don't think that's fair." A voice piped up. "Zuri corrected the factual misrepresentation in the presentation. If she hadn't done that, we would be in trouble with the client later."

Zuri exhaled. At least someone else had seen how off base the partner's comment was and said something about it. She was tired of living the reality where White workers who displayed anger were seen as having passion for their work, whereas workers of color were seen as "radical" or "not team players."[6] And she hadn't even expressed anger, she had simply made a factual correction to the data.

Misreading people, amplified by bias and internalized racism, means that perceptions spiral out of control and create additional difficulties, particularly in times of stress.[7] Our ability to spot bias and racism in action and our willingness to disrupt it in the moment is the long, often repetitive battle to weed out inequity and discrimination.

And bias doesn't just happen at work. It leaks out at times when we least expect it.

Jesse had been looking forward to the alumni miniature-golfing event all week. People that he hadn't seen for years would be there—some with their new significant others. He grabbed a drink from the concession stand and headed onto the course.

Waiting to take his turn, Jesse took a sip of his beer, and heard someone he didn't recognize remark, "I prefer the Irish to the Mexicans."

Jesse did a double take. Had someone really just said that? And what did the Irish or the Mexicans have to do with mini golf?

He said quickly, "What did you say?"

"Don't get up in arms. I was just talking about the beer," the person retorted.

"If you're just talking about the beer, say that you prefer Guinness to Modelo. There's no need to bring people and cultures into it."

Bias and jabs against people groups show up everywhere. Listening for how things might be interpreted and being willing to question things is a way to use our voices to create a kinder, more respectful world.

## Cultivate emotional culture

Alma dreaded talking with her brother Liam. They had both been champion debaters in school. Their parents had raised them to speak their minds, and as with many sibling rivalries, they both wanted to prove that they were as sharp and keen as anyone.

But each time her brother mentioned how poor people were lazy and how the government was wasting money trying to keep them alive, she felt fury. She gritted her teeth and geared up to battle. She pulled from new research and statistics. She looked at longevity studies and social impact. All the while, she grieved that any conversation with Liam would be fruitless.

Exhausted, the next time Alma was home and Liam started to argue, she stopped him. Alma looked her brother in the eye and said, "Look, as much as I love a good debate, I actually just want to be your sister. We don't need to be friends, but can we keep it civil? I don't want to leave every conversation feeling pummeled. I don't always want to have to be on guard with you."

Surprisingly, for the first time Alma could remember, Liam was quiet.

"I'll try," he said. "That's probably better for all of us."

Many people shy away from emotions. And yet emotional intelligence has been touted as the driving force of twenty-first-century business and what distinguishes top performers in every field.[8] We also know that people who feel safe and comfortable expressing their true feelings tend to be more productive, innovative, and creative.[9] Relationship—specifically focusing on emotions—serves as a way to use your voice. Noticing and expressing which emotions you are experiencing, and which others might be experiencing, is important, because emotions are information. If we're not paying attention to emotions, then we're missing out on data. Furthermore, the emotions people are allowed to share and that they feel the need to suppress define the emotional culture of an organization or family.[10] Failure to actively cultivate these expectations influences satisfaction, burnout, teamwork, and performance for everyone involved.

Isabel could hardly remember a time in her multidecade-long career when things had been more stressful. Sales were down, the company was burning through money faster than anticipated, and their competitors were already laying people off. As one of the few Hispanic CEOs of a multinational company, she felt the additional pressure to lead well, lest her handling of the situation be a reason why boards decide not to tap people who look like her for C-level roles in the future.

From experience, Isabel knew that saying nothing to employees would only make the situation worse. So at the next all-hands, she took a breath and said, "We know there's a lot of volatility in the world today. We are going to be as candid as we can about where we are at and what we're going to be doing. And through it all, we're going to live our company values of communication over efficiency, and humanity over utility."

Isabel couldn't control the economy, but she could steward the influence she had by naming how she intended to move through the challenges. Articulating the relationship you aspire to build can shape the emotional culture of a family, team, or community. As people, we will inevitably have our own strong opinions and reactions. Normalizing that we have, and can express, strong emotions sends the message that we can see things differently, navigate uncertainty, and still be human—together.

# Process

If substance is *what*, and relationship is *who*, process is *how*.

Process is all about how we go about work, love, and life. Process is whether there's an agenda for the meeting; whether and what is communicated before, during, and after a meeting; whether communication happens in real time or asynchronously, what medium we're using, who initiates and decides. Process is what mediators are specifically hired to manage, so that people can focus on the substance and relationship. *How* things are done has a huge impact on how people feel and what gets done. Process is the underrated lever for voice.

For Leila and the company she worked at, having thirty-five people on a call using different mediums contributes to people's silence by making it more difficult to speak up. People are less likely to speak up in large groups than small ones because there's more perceived social threat. We worry about social dynamics, what other people will think, and are busy evaluating ourselves compared to others.[11] That sets up incentives for people to observe rather than to engage, to seek safety in silence rather than say what they really think. From the outside, it seems obvious that a call with that many people would be far from productive, but too many organizations end up having such calls.

But process isn't just for the workplace.

I can't count the number of times that my loved ones and I were trying to figure out logistics for the weekend (substance). We're texting back and forth with typos trying to get through to each other (process). The answer is rarely to push forward, but to acknowledge that we're all wiped (relationship), and suggest we sleep on it and pick up the conversation in the morning (process), or if urgent, pick up the phone so we can talk in real time (process).

Process is the lever that allows us to design work and life in ways that better support our voices and the voices around us. Process allows us to reduce bias while minimizing the cognitive and emotional labor of calling things out. Process is the structure that can make it easier or harder for each of us to speak up. As a result, process affords a key opportunity to support voice. Below I'll explore five ways that you can use process to support your voice and the voices of those around you.

## Design intentionally

The best bachelorette weekend I ever attended included mandatory introvert time.

The organizer knew that the bride and everyone else could use a nap or downtime for a couple of hours between the morning hike and a fancy dinner. So she planned accordingly. It was the best nap I've ever taken. Everyone agreed that the intentionality of that plan allowed each of us to show up—and celebrate—fully.

Process is about designing the way we go about things in a way that nourishes each of us, so we can show up as the versions of ourselves we want to be. It's hard to move through the world when you are depleted. Rather than go about things the way they have been done or doing what you think you should do, consider what supports each of you—in the meeting, in a collaboration, and yes, even on a bachelorette weekend.

Too often the way conversations and interactions unfold is left to chance. We get people in a room and wing it, assuming that having the right people in the room leads to solutions. Gatherings and meetings without intentional design prioritize people who think on their feet or the preferences of the people with the most power in the dynamic. How conversations are structured fundamentally impacts which voices are amplified or silenced.

Anyone should be able to observe and comment on the infrastructure of an interaction. In Leila's case, it's likely that at an executive level, Sharath hasn't thought intentionally about meeting design and would be happy for someone else to figure out what would actually make the time productive. If Leila doesn't want to comment on substance or relationship, she can inquire as to whether everyone has access to the same notes, or note that the group hasn't taken a break in the last two hours and suggest they take one to improve everyone's engagement.

Better yet, she can have a one-to-one exchange with Sharath to make specific proposals about how the team could work better together. That conversation might sound something like: "Sharath, the thirty-five-people meetings aren't as productive as they could be. People are multitasking and not engaged. Having that many people on a call is also an expensive resource for the company and not conducive to the generative conversation I know you want to have. Here's what I propose. Let's reduce the number of people on the call, make sure everyone in attendance has a clear purpose and role, and I'll manage the communication of follow-on items to ensure information still flows to the entire team while freeing people up during regular meeting times. What do you think?"

Designing process is a specific way for each of us to use our voices to create the conditions that better support our own (and other) voices.

## DON'T LEAVE MEETINGS TO CHANCE

Process questions can seem so basic. Yet time and again, they are the ones that remain overlooked, especially as we jump from one meeting or task to another. Whether for a meeting, date, or community gathering, taking time to answer each of these questions ahead of time allows us to make conscious decisions about what will support people's voices rather than leaving voice to chance.

As you plan your time together, consider these questions—

- What preparation needs to happen to make the most of time and energy?
- What is the agenda or goal of the time together?
- What is a realistic length of time? What is an optimal time of day?
- Who is the decision maker? (If it's multiple people, who is the tiebreaker?)
- What medium (phone, email, video, in person, live, asynchronous) best supports the purpose or goal?
- What breaks are planned?
- What are the next steps?

## Suggest process moves that support your voice

We talked in chapter 5 about how choosing mediums that don't play to someone's strengths puts them at a disadvantage in the relationship and inclines them toward silence. The flip side of the idea is also true—to the extent possible, suggesting mediums and processes that play to your strengths is a way to support your own voice.

Many people have a preference for in-person, real-time communication. And it's true, both research and practice show that real-time conversation reduces the likelihood of confusion and can be more productive. Despite advances in technology, adults and children still process information and learn more effectively from live interactions rather than video-based communications. Adults in particular show poorer emotional fluency in video-based rather than live communication.[12]

At the same time, we all have different comfort levels with talking versus typing, real-time versus asynchronous communication. Time zones, geography, life circumstances, and our individual neurological wiring can make in-person or real-time conversations costly.

So when setting up a conversation or a meeting, consider the medium. What process choices play to your strengths and make it easier for you to use your voice?

I think best when I'm typing. Bullet points help me organize my thoughts. I think best when I have time to turn questions over rather than think on the spot, so I'll routinely ask people for questions and information ahead of time so I have time to metabolize the information and offer my best thinking. While it can take marginally more effort and planning to identify questions and communicate them ahead of time, doing so means you capture more insight than the dominant voices alone offer. Working remotely, I spend much of my life on video calls. But I regularly suggest phone rather than video calls when we don't need to be looking at a document, so that I can walk outside while we talk. The fresh air, change of scenery, and increased blood flow ultimately help me be more present.

Do you know what mediums, practices, and rhythms best support the voices of those around you? If not, let them know you're curious about their preferences for the next time you connect.

## Be explicit about implicit norms

Can people share thoughts by chat or do they have to speak verbally? Do you have to raise your virtual or physical hand before you speak in a meeting? Should people ask questions along the way or wait until the end of the presentation? Most people want to play by the rules, but doing so requires knowing what the rules are. Making the implicit explicit helps everyone understand the expectations around voice.

Charlene had learned to wait until called on, because when she spoke out of turn, her last manager shot her a look that was now seared in her brain. She didn't want to be rude or interrupt. At her new job, she assumed that her new manager would invite questions and comments after he presented the latest plan, so she waited her turn. But he didn't. He assumed that if people had something to say, they would speak up.

Her communication within her homeowners association was equally frustrating. When the common area needed electrical work, she gathered and shared proposals from contractors, asking folks to weigh in before the board hired someone. She worried that if she didn't get sign-off from everyone, homeowners would come back and raise hell with her. It wasn't until an old-timer told her that if you don't hear back from anyone, it means they are okay with whatever you decide that she gave up chasing people down and hired a contractor.

Absent clarity, people are left to read the tea leaves of what the rules are and default to the norms they are used to. Making norms explicit is one way to use process to guard against the default patterns that disproportionately silence people who hold less power in the system and to reduce friction and frustration.

## Have standard questions

We know from earlier chapters that it is hard to oppose authority. There's a lot at stake when expressing opposition, especially to someone who holds more systemic power than you do. Yet we also know that we need different perspectives to help us avoid costly mistakes and see the world more clearly. Process can help build space for opposition (and reduce the personal risks to sharing opposition) by building the invitation for dissenting views into the process. Having standard questions that everyone knows to expect invites and depersonalizes opposition. Complementary questions allow you to evaluate an issue and solve for positivity bias.

Complementary questions include:

- What about this works? What about this doesn't work? (And why?)
- What are the pros of the idea? What are the cons?
- What are the upsides? What are the downsides?

For example, if you disagree with your boss at work, it may not be acceptable to tell them directly that they are wrong. Instead, you may rely on standardized questions to reveal how you disagree and discuss why. Similarly, in personal relationships, having questions you both know to expect and answer keeps opinions focused on evaluating the issue at hand, rather than someone's preferences or character.

Taking the train rather than driving to get to a destination.

Dusty-blue instead of cornflower-blue paint for the accent wall. Whether to eliminate a position in an organization.

All these situations processed through a set of standard questions depersonalizes the analysis and invites people into a conversation. Whatever the specific language that fits your context and culture, the goal is to have a grouping of questions that teases out both the positive and the negative, what's working and what's not working. Standard questions help surface opposition by baking opposition into the questions that the group wrestles with rather than placing the burden on any one individual to raise an issue.

## Tend to procedural justice

For Danielle, Christmas was the most magical time of year. She had such lovely memories of decorating the house and tree with her family. Her mother made the best spiced apple cider as Christmas carols played and multicolored lights twinkled. Christmas in her childhood home was worthy of TV, except better because it was real life.

When things got serious with Adam, Danielle knew there would be compromises. But Christmas at her parents' home was one thing she did not want to let go of. Adam agreed they would do Thanksgiving with his family and Christmas with hers. After all, Thanksgiving was a more important tradition in his family than Christmas.

But when Christmas rolled around, Adam insisted they spend it with his folks. "My parents are older than yours. We have fewer Christmases left with them," he reasoned. Plus, his nieces really wanted Uncle Adam to read them *A Christmas Story* on Christmas morning, as he had every year of their lives.

"We can do Christmas morning with the kids and then drive to your folks' in time for Christmas dinner," he argued.

Danielle fumed. Spending half of Christmas Day driving through wintry mix wasn't Christmas. Getting to wake up in her childhood home to the smell of Nana's gingerbread French toast and strong coffee was Christmas. Plus, Adam had promised she could have Christmas if he got Thanksgiving.

Adam refused to give in. They both stewed on the issue for weeks.

Finally, the day of, Adam agreed. We'll drive down to your parents' in time for Christmas Eve dinner, he said.

Danielle would be at her parents' house, but she still wasn't happy about how everything had played out. Why had Adam put her through that agony? Why had he gone back on his word? Why had he ruined the entire holiday season with his stubbornness?

During the drive, Danielle was quiet. She was trying to shift as quickly as she could from the bitterness and rage into Christmas joy. *You got what you wanted in the end, Danielle,* she told herself. *Why are you still bitter about it?*

*How* we get to decisions and go through life matters. Procedural justice is the fairness of the process rather than the outcome. People are more likely to accept outcomes if they also believe the process is fair.[13] In Danielle's case, even if the outcome was the one that she originally wanted, the lack of fairness in *how* they got to the decision still erodes trust and relationship.

Process decisions can either support silence or voice. Make process decisions that best support your voice, and pay attention to what processes support voice for the people you impact.

THERE IS NO ONE WAY TO USE YOUR VOICE. EACH OF OUR VOICES will look and sound different from others'. The question is, Where and when do *you* want to use your voice?

When I'm not getting the outcomes I want, I doubt whether I'm using my voice effectively. In those moments, I remind myself—and you—that as much as we might wish it to be, voice is not a once-and-done instance. Using our voices to influence the people and the world around us is an ongoing process. Substance, relationship, and process give us more levers to pull when we're questioning how to use our voices.

Given the silence we've learned, muscles for voice are under-developed in many of us. Each time we choose silence, we reinforce the reflexive habits we've developed for silence and miss out on an opportunity to develop the muscle for using our voice. Each time we choose voice is an opportunity to build our muscles to express different opinions, listen across differences, and challenge injustice. There's no guarantee that we'll come out of using our voices unscathed. But with exercise, rest, and nourishment, our muscles for voice strengthen.

These days, it's far easier for me to ask taxi drivers to change the temperature in the car. I've renegotiated boundaries with colleagues so I don't have to keep having the same conversation on repeat. I've learned that "no" can be a complete sentence because no is what allows me to care for myself. Being able to use my voice hasn't been without bumps and emergency texts to friends who remind me that I'm not ridiculous for advocating for what I care about.

But each time I speak up, I'm consciously unlearning silence and learning to use my voice.

# YOUR TURN

---

Identify a situation where you want to use your voice.
For example, a group project at work, a tricky dynamic
between family members, or a social issue you care about.

## What is your take on the **substance**?

- What aspects of the substance are in your domain?

- What perspective do you bring?

## How can you tend to the **relationship**?

- Which people or people groups are impacted by this
  situation?

- What biases might be at play?

- What emotions are you feeling?

- How might other people be feeling?

## What **process** will best support your (and others') voice?

- How can you intentionally design the process?

- What process choices best support your own voice?

- What implicit norms do you need to make explicit?

- What standard questions can you ask?

- What do you need to do to make the process feel fair?

# 8

# How to Speak Up

n the early days of living together, my husband and I had a conversation I've fondly come to refer to as Toiletgate. It was a typical weekend of trying to take care of the things that don't happen during the workweek.

Taking stock of what we had to do, I commented, "We should really clean the toilet today."

"But I already cleaned it," he replied.

I'm sure I furrowed my brow as I thought of the current state of the toilet. I didn't want to be a nag, but to me, the toilet was most certainly not clean.

"If you cleaned it, why are there still yellow streaks on the outside?" I asked, befuddled.

"Why would you clean the outside of the toilet? It's not the part that anyone uses," he replied matter-of-factly.

I was shocked. I had never thought *not* to clean the outside of the toilet. I had watched my mom clean the base and bowl, and I myself had cleaned the toilet interior and exterior my entire life. The outside was where the dust and grime collected, especially when urine splashes back or users of the toilet who shall remain unnamed miss in the middle of the night.

At the same time, I could see why my husband would think that the exterior wasn't the part people used. The purpose of the base is to hold up the bowl, which holds up the seat. Most of us can go through life without touching the base of the toilet.

But my mind flashed forward—if one day we have a kid crawling around in the phase when they are exploring the world by putting things in their mouth, the kid couldn't possibly be exposed to a yellow-streaked, dust-covered toilet base. As much as I wanted to share all this with my husband, I remained speechless—unable to untangle my bewilderment from my confusion and concern.

WHETHER AT WORK OR AT HOME, PEOPLE HAVE LONG TOLD ME TO just speak up. But we know speaking up is not as easy as flipping a switch or reciting a script. I'm aware, as we explored in the previous chapter, that I can rely on substance, relationship, and process to use my voice. Those levers help me design a path for using my voice and serve as handholds in the moment. But there are times—like in the midst of Toiletgate—when I open my mouth, nothing comes out.

Whether speaking up about hygiene or inequity, I want to be able to speak up for what I believe is right. I want to be able to add my perspective to what is going on. I want to be able to comment on the substance, and not just rely on relationship or process. (Did you know that the average toilet seat is covered in about 295 bacteria per square inch,[1] and one flush produces thousands of aerosol droplets containing bacteria and viruses that can contaminate surfaces up to six feet away?[2] Okay, that's the end of the toilet talk. But I was right to be concerned!)

In situations where you are flabbergasted, speechless, or shocked, what do you actually say, and how do you get yourself in a place where you can actually have words and meaning come out of your mouth?

In this chapter, I offer four anchors based on the pitfalls I've observed in my own life speaking up and in years spent coaching others to speak up.

In order to speak up in those moments when we don't know what to say, we need to 1) start with why, 2) connect the dots, 3) make the ask clear, and 4) embrace resistance. The four anchors provide a template for preparing to speak up and knowing what you need to cover when you open your mouth, so that others are more likely to hear and understand you. Like an anchor used to keep a boat from drifting away due to winds or currents, each of these anchors helps us stay the course on what we want to communicate, even when people distract us or change the tenor, topic, or context of the conversation.

## Start with Why

Author Simon Sinek popularized the idea of starting with why as a fundamental business principle. In order to get buy-in from your teams, motivate others, and achieve most anything, you have to start with why. He points to research that shows that starting with why maps with the engagement of our brains, as why resonates not just with the neocortex, but with the limbic system.[3] Why provides emotional context for making decisions.

The same goes for understanding why we want to use our voices. What's in it for me—long known by the acronym WIIFM—captures the idea that there has to be something in it for each of us in order for us to pay attention. So many things clamor for our attention that we need some hook in order to know why we ought to listen to anyone else. Is the suggestion going to help people think better of me? Allow us to collaborate more effectively across functions? Reduce pain going forward? People are more likely to listen and respond favorably if they understand why the idea you're sharing matters—or should matter—to them.

But knowing why isn't just for the people you're trying to reach. Fundamentally, knowing why we're speaking up is key for each of us. Why would we put ourselves through the gauntlet of calculations, risks, and possible consequences of speaking up if there wasn't something—a why—that mattered more to us than the risk and discomfort?

We need something to anchor to, to remind us why we'd put ourselves through it and take the risks. What is more important to you than your own discomfort, that makes the energy and investment worth it? Whether or not you articulate the bigger why—or which why—to others, connecting to a bigger reason gives you clarity as to why you'd lend your voice to this context and situation. *Why* gives you an answer to the question: Is it worth it to speak up?

According to psychologist Robert Kegan and Harvard lecturer on education Lisa Lahey, in order to change, you need something that matters more to you than the old behavior.[4] If you're going to lose weight, you have to have a compelling reason to do so. You have to care more about your health or being able to run around with your grandkids than continuing the same patterns that contributed to your current weight. If silence is the old behavior, the known habit, what is it that matters more to each of us that makes it worth it to speak up?

Human dignity.

Justice.

Belonging.

A shot at a promotion.

Knowing that we tried.

Love—for self or others.

Nicola had been navigating nerve pain for years. Some days, the pain shot down her back, as if someone was stabbing her repeatedly. Other days, the pain in her hands was so sharp that she couldn't hold her coffee mug. Nicola had good days, when the pain felt manageable. Then all of sudden, a burning sensation would spread like wildfire through her legs. In those moments, all she could do was cling to her pillow, curl up in a ball, and will the pain to pass.

She had seen different doctors, but no one had answers. She tried ice, heat, ointments, diets, pills—even acupuncture—but nothing seemed to help.

Other than physical pain, what was most gut-wrenching to Nicola was how little people around her could empathize with what was going on. Initially, family and friends would look at her with concern, then pity. After a while, they started asking whether she was making the pain up. *You look fine from the outside and there's no blood. You really can't hold a cup?* When she winced at the dinner table, her husband gave her a look as if to communicate that she shouldn't be so dramatic.

On the worst days, Nicola couldn't get out of bed. She had energetic six- and eight-year-old kids. Who was going to take care of them?

Nicola's mother-in-law, Isis, offered to help. With Nicola out on unpaid medical leave from her job, Nicola's husband was the sole breadwinner for the family. And Isis hated seeing the family stretched so thin.

Having Isis around was a lifesaver. She was mostly great with the kids, and could take care of meals, cleaning, and making sure the kids got to and from school.

But what stung were the comments Nicola heard through the walls.

"That wife of yours is useless. In my day, if we were sick we would still push on."

"She made herself sick with all that vegan business. She just isn't getting enough protein."

"Why didn't you marry someone who was stronger? We warned you she would be trouble."

At first, Nicola tried to ignore the cutting remarks. After all, Isis was helping them out. Nicola told herself she could be the bigger person and let it go. She didn't have to like her mother-in-law. Nicola wasn't even surprised that her husband had stayed silent. They had been married long enough for her to know that it was unlikely he would defend her. Her husband had never been able to push back against his mother, and he certainly wasn't going to work out four decades of his own childhood trauma before dinner.

But the more Nicola thought about it, the more it seemed like something needed to be said. If her husband wouldn't say something, she would need to. Even if she could hardly get out of bed, she still deserved to be treated as a human being—especially in her own home. If she could hear her mother-in-law's put-downs, her kids certainly could hear them too. What then, would they think of their own mother? Dignity, respect, and how she wanted her kids to treat others were reason enough for Nicola to speak up.

Like Nicola, it's helpful to identify your bigger why before you speak or act. You may already intuitively know what it is, but articulating your why to yourself—and deciding whether to share it with the other person—helps you orient yourself, even when the waves of doubt hit.

## Connect the Dots

Based on our life experience, situation, and vantage point, we all have access to different information and are going to process data differently. But it's not until moments like Toiletgate that we are reminded of *how* differently we all think.

Originally from Oman, Khajeer had been working for an import-export business for years. When he was hired, the Australian founders had promised that if he put in the hours and proved his worth, they would make him a partner in the business. They constantly said things like, "Khajeer, we couldn't do all of this without you." But as years went by, the founders never did the paperwork to make him an official partner. Khajeer wondered if it would ever happen.

Whenever he asked about when he would be made a partner, there was always a reason for the delay—family health issues, a demanding client, a different priority. Khajeer wanted to believe the people he was working with, but each day that passed made it harder for him to trust that change would happen.

Wanting to assume the best about the partners, Khajeer decided to connect the dots for them, saying, "I have worked here for nine years. You told me that after six years, you would make me a partner. I know there is a lot going on, but I also know that there is always something happening. Every time you say that you'll make me partner soon and then don't, the less I trust that you'll keep your word. I feel like my choices are to accept things as they are, or to quit. As an immigrant to this country—if you don't have your papers, you can always get kicked out. To me, it's the same with this company. Unless the partnership is official—and even if it is—you still hold the power to kick me out. That's not a risk I can continue to take."

More often than not, people have a reaction similar to mine when my husband explained why he didn't need to clean the entire toilet—something like "Oh, I had never thought of it that way." Connecting the dots can be an opportunity for people—like Khajeer's colleagues—to understand the impact of their choices and behavior. It's an opportunity for them to understand the unintended consequences of their actions. Most well-meaning people don't like being seen showing up as anything less than the well-meaning people we all think we are.

Connecting the dots is an opportunity to help others see what might not otherwise be visible to them, and share the logical connections that you see from your perspective. It is a way of showing someone else that there is a different way of thinking about the situation—allowing them to understand the meaning you're making.

## Make the Ask Clear

We might hope that after connecting the dots, people would be able to follow the throughline and know what to do differently going forward. But experience has shown me that leaving the ask to chance is a recipe for further miscommunication and frustration. Much like the friend who is offering solutions when the other person just wants them to listen, or the manager who is not providing enough direction to team members on a project because they don't want to micromanage, intuiting what others are asking of us is a hard job to do well. Making clear what we are asking of people allows them to make informed decisions about whether to accept or reject our requests.

In Toiletgate, I wish I had made the ask explicit: "Could we agree going forward that in our family, cleaning the toilet means that we clean both the inside and outside of the toilet bowl and base?" It can feel demeaning, or elementary, to have to spell it out. Yet not having spelled the standard out is what gets us into Toiletgates in the first place.

And I'm not the only one who can benefit from the clarity.

Catalina wasn't sure what to do. The community group that she had founded was splintering. Instead of working together, people were fighting with each other. No one could agree on what issues to tackle and how to get the word out in the community.

Her friends suggested she reach out to Gerrit, as he was a well-regarded, experienced community organizer who had navigated many of the gnarly dynamics she now faced.

After weeks of playing phone tag, she was finally able to catch him on the phone and shared her situation.

"What would you do?" she asked.

To Catalina's dismay, Gerrit replied, "Trust yourself. You'll know what to do."

Seriously? That's all he had? She had held off making any decisions, hoping to find a useful thought partner in Gerrit and some tactical strategies for what to do. While the empathy was nice, it felt like being back at square one.

Gerrit noticed her silence. "What's wrong?"

"I'm actually looking for advice."

"Don't women just want to be listened to?"

"I mean, sure. Sometimes. But today I want and need tactical advice. If you were me, what would you do? You've run organizations before. You've had to let people go before. You've analyzed risk before. I'm not asking you to tell me what to do, I'm asking you to share what you might do."

The mismatch between what we want from others and what

others think we want from them is all too common. Being clear what we are looking for from the other person allows us to give them a clear role to play. While asking for what we want can be difficult, the clarity that ensues helps well-intended efforts not miss the mark.

So, before you make your next ask, consider these questions. Do you want someone to hear you out? To be a thought partner? To allow you to vent but not fix the problem? To offer solutions to the problem? Being explicit about what you're looking for from the other person allows them to make an informed decision as to whether it's a role they can play. More often than not, people want to be helpful but simply don't know how to show up in the moment. Giving them an explicit role helps them know what will be helpful to *you*.

## Embrace Resistance

Starting with why, connecting the dots, and making clear asks all help manage the resistance we inevitably encounter when we use our voice. As much as you may speak your mind, others can (and will) have their own reactions.

But their reactions don't have to negate your voice. Instead of seeing others' resistance as a reason to stay silent, know that resistance is a normal part of the process and embrace it.

Vitali was an associate on the Reporting and Analytics team at an investment firm. Knowing that the chief data officer and others had far more experience than he did, Vitali was hesitant to share his idea about how the firm could streamline their processes. But he had also been told that to work his way up in the firm, he'd have to differentiate himself from all the other worker bees.

So in the next team meeting, when leadership asked if anyone had anything else to add, Vitali made his suggestion. "If we can use this platform to go from raw data to visualization in minutes, that would be a win for our clients."

The criticism arrived almost immediately from multiple people.

"That will never work."

"It's not that easy."

"What about data security issues?"

Vitali was shaken. What had happened to "We're open to all suggestions for process improvement"? Or that you would be rewarded for novel ideas? Apparently that was all just corporate bullshit. Vitali returned to his desk deflated.

So often we bristle at criticism. People's opinions of us or our work can feel deeply personal and incredibly demotivating. The social threat we experience when we're met with resistance rather than receptivity is real. And yet, resistance is a natural and useful part of expressing ideas and engaging with one another.

Criticism is a form of engagement, even if it is not the way we would prefer someone to engage with us. Resistance contains information that can be useful for getting to a better outcome. Specifically, issue raising is one of the ways that ideas are cultivated within a team. Because 80 percent of our work these days takes place in the context of teams or groups of people, speaking up and presenting issues to the group is particularly important.[5] As discouraging as it is to have someone call out a weakness in your idea or to question your judgment, their resistance creates an opportunity for others to engage further and propose different solutions to keep the idea alive.

As the day went on, the more Vitali thought about the conversation, the more motivated he became. In his next one-to-one, he asked his manager, "If we could solve the data security issue, is this something the firm would be interested in?" Of course. The end result would be a win. But right now, no one knows how to get there.

Knowing that resistance is a natural part of voice helps us be less triggered by it. Instead of getting caught up in the frustration of feeling criticized or rejected, we can embrace resistance by acknowledging that, however frustrating, it is a part of the process.

It's worth noting that having a strong backup plan is the not-so-secret factor that makes it far easier to weather someone's resistance. BATNA—best alternative to a negotiated agreement—is the classic negotiation term for what you will do if the other person can't agree to something that works for you. A common negotiation pitfall is assuming that you don't have any alternatives, which simply isn't true. Our alternatives might not be great, but remembering that you have a BATNA and actively working to improve what seems like the best of those alternatives gives you leverage, even if you don't end up choosing the alternative.

For Nicola suffering from nerve pain, she might feel that accepting Isis's help—alongside the healthy dose of her mother-in-law's opinions—is her only option. After all, their family is now a one-income household and finding other cost-effective help would be challenging. But if Nicola can line up another family member or a series of friends who could help, then she would feel far less beholden to her mother-in-law.

If Isis is able to change her behavior after hearing Nicola share her perspective and understand what Nicola is asking of her, then it could be a good outcome for her to remain part of the day-to-day care team. But if Isis is unable or unwilling to stop with the hurtful remarks, then Nicola has other ways of covering the day-to-day childcare and household tasks that Isis is helping them with, with less emotional and relational pain in the mix.

Speaking up always takes place in the shadow of our alternatives—the stronger our BATNA, the less we have to worry about the other person's willingness to listen or comply. After all, you know that there is something you *could* do, even if your mother-in-law bails on you.

Using your voice can feel like two steps forward, one step back, sideways, and upside down. But understanding that resistance is part of the process, that resistance contains valuable information that could inform your next steps, and that you have and can improve your alternative helps you from getting thrown off-kilter as much.

MANY OF US WANT SPEAKING UP AND USING OUR VOICES TO BE once-and-done instances. Life would certainly be far less exhausting if that were the case. Unfortunately, it is rarely so. Voice is a collective, interactional process rather than a one-time event between two people who exist in their own bubble.[6]

Starting with why, connecting the dots, making clear asks, and embracing resistance provide four anchors to reach for and rely on as the waves of opinion and criticism—and, well, life—come your way. Using these four anchors to prepare for when you want to speak up means that you will be prepared to engage in a productive way. Keeping these anchors in mind during a conversation means that you always have a steady idea to grasp on to when you want to engage on the substance. With these four anchors, I hope you'll speak up so we can all benefit from your ideas, insight, and inspiration.

Speaking up is not a solo act. So in the next chapter, we turn to how we can stop silencing each other and instead support each other's voices so none of us have to go it alone.

# YOUR TURN

---

Which of these four anchors do you tend to use intuitively?

Which of these anchors could you add to your tool kit the next time you need to speak up?

What is a situation where you want to speak up?

### 1. Start with why

*What is the reason that you would want to speak up?*

"This is about safety."

### 2. Connect the dots

*What is your thought process?*

"Here's what I'm seeing . . . I'm concerned that . . ."

### 3. Make the ask clear

*What are you asking of the other person(s)?*

"I want to be able to make a decision together on this."

### 4. Embrace resistance

*Remember, their resistance is normal. Ask questions to understand why they are hesitant, opposed, or concerned.*

"What concerns . . . ?"

# 9

# Stop Silencing People

Walking back to the van, Scarlett was furious. After everyone had climbed in and closed the doors, she took a deep breath and said to her friends, "Y'all are lucky the people in that restaurant are nicer than you are. Everyone could hear you making jokes—about rednecks, about hunting, about hicks and hillbillies. About them. And about me." Scarlett is a White woman who had grown up in rural West Virginia before moving to New York to pursue her big-city dreams. "Stereotypes go both ways. That was so rude. You are lucky people had compassion and grace for you today."

The van ride away from the Waffle House was silent for a long while before her friend Rick spoke up.

He said, "I'm really sorry. I know how it feels to have people make assumptions about me just because I'm Brown. You're right. I should have known better."

"Do better next time," Scarlett clapped back. "Because when you profile and stereotype them, you're just as bad as the people who profile and stereotype you. Have some respect."

WE SILENCE PEOPLE. I DO IT. YOU DO IT.

To be clear, most of the time when we silence people, we do so unintentionally. We typically see ourselves as caring and supportive. We want the people around us to feel seen, known, and heard. We want to create cultures in which their—and our—humanity shines. We want people to thrive. But often we don't have the impact we intend.

This chapter is about how we can make our good intentions reality. You'll learn how to be aware and conscious of how you are showing up, so there's less collateral damage.

We can stop silencing people by listening across differences, clearing preconceived notions, centering others' interests and agency (instead of our own), normalizing differences, and making rules discussable. Adopting each of the behaviors from this chapter will make it easier for you to show up as the caring and supportive person you intend, and for the people around you to choose voice rather than silence.

## Listen, Especially Across Difference

Dominican-born Amara was hard-pressed to remember a time she had seen eye to eye with her manager, Maggie, who had grown up and still lived in a wealthy White suburb. Whenever Amara asked a question, Maggie would reply, "I don't want to tell you what to do, but when I was in your role . . ."

Months went by when every suggestion Amara made was met with the same feedback. Despite being promised that she would have autonomy in her role, Amara was expected to be a mini-Maggie, doing all the same things in exactly the same way.

The problem was, the way Maggie had done things wasn't working. A big part of Amara's job was to fundraise, but the strategies Maggie approved weren't inspiring donors to contribute. Amara felt like she had to say something. "Maggie, we're still coming up short of our fundraising goal. We need a different approach."

When Maggie paused, Amara was hopeful. But then Maggie said, "Amara, I can appreciate your enthusiasm to try something new. But if you're not getting results, it's because you're not following the plan."

Amara felt defeated. A few days later, she got an email from HR. Maggie said that Amara was creating a toxic work environment and needed to work on her collaboration skills. Amara felt stuck—Maggie's strategy didn't work, but she wasn't allowed to try anything different. Clearly, Amara was damned if she spoke up and damned if she didn't.

What was she to do?

Most of us know viscerally what it's like to say something and have the message go unheard, and to be told we're wrong or off base. Not being heard inclines us toward silence.

We're also guilty of not listening to others, especially when we disagree with what they are saying or they aren't communicating to us in our preferred style.

Instead of listening, we complete their sentences for them.

We assume, we rebut, we tune out, we project.

We silence—even when we're going through the motions of listening. And as a result, we miss out on the information and perspective being offered to us to solve problems, and deny others' dignity in the process.

"Listen" is such common advice that it is almost hard to hear. Ninety-six percent of people self-identify as good listeners.[1] Yet moments after sitting through a ten-minute oral presentation, half of adults can't describe the contents of the presentation. Forty-eight hours later, 75 percent of listeners can't recall the subject matter of the presentation.[2]

Leaders like Maggie often ignore or reject what is said if they feel threatened, have implicit negative beliefs and biases about those in lower-power roles, have inflated self-assessed competence, or all of the above.[3] When we respond to opinions with resistance or denial, for whatever reason, people rightfully conclude that speaking up is not worth the risk.[4] Yet ignoring or rejecting what people say does no favors. Being heard is necessary for solving problems, working together, and being able to coexist without constantly annoying the heck out of each other.[5] Silencing others gets in the way of what most of us want.

The research is also clear that people are more likely to voice concerns and experience psychological safety when authority holders are perceived as open, approachable, responsive, empowering, and inclusive.[6] Can Maggie hold her own opinion *and* work to understand what things look like from where Amara sits? After all, warnings don't always come with flashing neon signs and ear-splitting alarms. If Maggie remains closed off to Amara's observations of what's not working, the team won't meet their fundraising goal. If she can hear what Amara is saying, the team could change their strategy and at least have a chance.

Unless we can create spaces where people are confident their contributions are valued, we are inclining people toward silence rather than voice. Being able to listen—especially across differences—is the first step to building and maintaining space where voice is welcome. After all, warnings often come in the form of uncomfortable conversations where people are telling us what we don't want to hear. Our responses in the moment determine whether we get—or miss out on—that information.

So what does listening and being able to hear across difference look like?

Listening means working to understand what the other person is trying to communicate, which may or may not be reflected in the words they initially use. As you listen, ask yourself: What is the core of what they are trying to convey? What are they really saying or asking?

Check your motivation and purpose at the moment. Are you listening just to confirm your own understanding of the world, or listening for the intent and heart of what the individual is trying to express? Listening, not to rebut or defend, but to understand and make the other person feel heard, is what supports voice.

Amara's concern that she won't be able to accomplish the department's objectives with the current resources should be met with inquiry and curiosity. If Maggie shuts Amara down, what happens? Amara gets that email, stays silent so she doesn't continue creating a "toxic" environment, fails to meet her goals, and burns out because she didn't have the resources to do her job. The org still loses.

To cultivate voice rather than silence, Maggie would ask Amara to share more about the concern rather than telling her to make it work. If Maggie were listening, she would hear and acknowledge that, from where Amara sits, repeating past plans doesn't work. Maggie would work to understand why Amara sees it differently than she does. Maggie might ask, What do you think has changed since last year? What do you need from me? Working to understand Amara's concerns doesn't mean that Maggie has to agree with them.

But silencing Amara doesn't make the problem go away—silence just kicks the problem down the line and often makes things worse.

## Clear Preconceived Notions

In addition to hearing what folks have to say, we can support voice by clearing the preconceived notions we—and others—might hold about them.

If Scarlett's friends were honest, they had made fun of locals in the Waffle House because *they* were deeply uncomfortable thousands of miles from the urban oases they called home. Scarlett's friends were conscious that their designer jeans and white sneakers stuck out amid the camo and orange that the regulars wore. They weren't comfortable that all eyes were on them as they walked in, even though they were the ones entering someone else's home turf. They assumed that the locals were mocking them for being coastal elites, even though they didn't exchange a word with anyone other than the server, who had been nothing but respectful and friendly toward them.

It was easier for Scarlett's friends to criticize the people they didn't know—and assumed didn't vote like them—than to be curious about what life was like in a place very different from where they called home.

In the van, Scarlett continued. "Look, I grew up in a double-wide. My neighbors had never left the state, much less this country. But they were kind people who always lent a hand."

After a long pause, Rick asked, "What's a double-wide?"

"A double-wide is a mobile home. A trailer," Scarlett responded. "To me, it was just home. It's what my folks could afford. And they made sure my brothers and I had what we needed."

There was quiet in the van as Scarlett's friends saw her—and the communities they were driving through—in a new light. This was still the Scarlett they knew and loved. The Scarlett who ordered bottle service when they hit the clubs and could MacGyver them out of any sticky situation. It was the same Scarlett who would debate the merits of stock options in comp packages and would not put up with anyone's shit, a survival skill she had learned as the first in her family to go to college.

Scarlett had made her point. Her friends realized that just because someone was from the country didn't make them backward. As they drove past horse farms and grassland, she continued to explain that hunting was a way parents and their kids could connect and have quality time doing a shared activity. Just like Rick's family had done puzzles together on their dining-room table. The conversation reminded Scarlett's friends that they all were just people. The folks eating smothered and covered hash browns were just parents trying to provide for their kids.

We all make assumptions about people based on what we think we know about them. We hold preconceived notions about people based on the color of their skin, what school they went to, how much money we think they have.

The way to support someone's voice starts with seeing them as unique individuals rather than the stereotypes, biases, and impressions you (and others) hold toward the identities they carry. Figure out who they are and support their voice by clearing rather than reinforcing the preconceived notions others might have about them.

## Center Their Interests and Agency

Having been at this architecture firm for two years, Erik was now one of the old-timers. He'd seen people come and go. He'd seen the double standards that colleagues who didn't look like the White leadership faced, and he wanted to disrupt them. When the last employee of color submitted his resignation, Erik vowed never to let it happen again. Going forward, he would no longer be silent about injustice.

When a new employee joined the team, Erik noticed they were taking on more work than any other person. He jumped in. Erik worried that, like those who came before them, the new employee would face the hurdles of inequity within the system. Concerned about whether the team member was being treated fairly, Erik wrote the team lead asking them to reduce the new employee's workload because they were getting more than their share of tasks and duties.

Erik was proud that he had sounded the alarm.

Clara, the team lead, was confused. She met with the new employee every week and had been keeping a close eye on workload to avoid the same situation that Erik was worried about. She had been intentionally building an open and trusting relationship with the new team member. When they met yesterday, the new team member had said they were comfortable with the workload and, in fact, were excited to have a range of different experiences. So where was Erik's information coming from?

Clara thanked Erik for his concern and promised to look into the situation.

When she approached the new employee, saying that others were concerned about the workload, the new employee was just as confused. "We talked about workload yesterday," he said. "I agreed that the load was good and appreciated the mix of different projects. Why are we talking about this again?"

As we work to use our voices to champion the things we believe, we are bound to miss the mark. One key way of supporting others' voices is to center their needs, wants, goals, desires, and perspectives, rather than our own.

Erik could have asked the new employee what they thought about the workload before going to the team lead. "I'm seeing that your calendar is full. To me, that schedule would be too much. How is the workload sitting with you?" Or, had Erik said, "I know it's hard to be new, and I want to do what I can to help. My inclination is to raise the issue with Clara so that you don't have to. Is that actually helpful?" the new employee could have redirected his good intentions.

Before jumping into action on someone's behalf or for a cause, check to make sure your information is good. What rubs us the wrong way might be okay—or not worth raising—for someone else differently situated. Don't assume that you know what would be best for the other person. Instead, ask what would help them thrive. Does this person want your involvement? How can you actually be most supportive of them? Taking action to speak on their behalf without inquiring whether it's helpful likely creates more challenges for them, despite your good intentions.

We all thrive under different circumstances. What do the people around you need? What conditions best support the voices of those around you? Where are they on their own journey of cultivating and using their voice? Do they need the spotlight? Do they need an affirming nudge that they have something worthy to say? When in doubt, let them know your intention to support them. You can either ask how you can best support them or share your inclination with them so they have an opportunity to tell you if it actually helps support their voice.

In short, supporting someone means letting their needs and preferences drive the way you show up rather than defaulting to your own needs and preferences.

## HOW TO DO YOUR OWN WORK

Have you heard the phrase "Do your own work" but not known what it really means? Doing your own work means developing awareness of how your own life experiences shape your biases, prejudices, assumptions, and actions—and figuring out how you want to let those experiences shape life going forward.

For most of us, doing our own work includes being aware of the different types of physical or emotional trauma we've experienced and finding ways to heal so that we don't inflict that same pain on the people around us. Our work involves educating ourselves about the things that didn't make it into the curriculum at the schools we attended or the conversations at our dinner tables. It includes processing our defensive and triggered reactions on our own time—not with the people impacted by our actions. It means sitting in the discomfort of knowing we've been complicit and wrestling with the ways we've contributed. Doing our work means getting out of the swirl of guilt and shame to get to constructive action that centers the needs of those we've traditionally marginalized. At times, it means doing the work that is yours to do and letting others do theirs.

Until we do our own work, it's difficult to center someone else's interests effectively. By doing our own work, we are able to identify whether a strong reaction is about us, another person, or the situation. It's important to do the work with people similarly situated. Don't do your work with your team or direct report, or across lines of lower power. Instead, talk with a friend, a coach, or your manager. Making the people impacted by your actions sit through your processing in real time further centers your own needs and silences their voice.

# Normalize Different Styles of Communication

My friend and I used to be able to go for coffee on a whim. We'd soak up the freedom of not having plans or being responsible for anyone but ourselves. We'd take spontaneous trips together because we could.

These days, life looks a lot different. She sends me audio messages that she records while breastfeeding. I sneak-text back from the checkout line at the grocery store before doing pickup.

Weeks often pass between our exchanges. We've agreed that there's no guilt or obligation to reply. We understand that life is full with all the different roles and responsibilities we each hold. Audio messages aren't my preferred mode of communication; texts aren't hers. But we're both grateful that the connection remains.

There's often a gold standard of communication—a single way of communicating that is most prized.

In person.

No *umm*s.

Clear, crisp, and to the point.

Look the person in the eye.

Respond in a timely manner.

Show enough emotion to seem authentic, but not enough to make people uncomfortable.

These norms—and so many more—assume White corporate orientation, high education level, and neurotypicality. They mean that people for whom these aren't the defaults need to contort themselves to fit a mold before they can be heard. Those for whom English is a second language have yet another layer to worry about other than just learning the words. It means that the voices of those who communicate more effectively by writing or typing are not given as much value as those who can smooth talk.

Voice is messy. Life is full of *umm*s. Can we normalize different modes and means of expression?

I realize I'm making a big ask. Because it's a lot easier to hear someone when they are communicating in our preferred way, at our preferred time, and ideally, expressing views we want to hear. But only being able to hear people who cater to our preferred mode of receiving information means that we are skewing the data we curate. We are creating additional barriers of entry and engagement based on the communication norms of the people already in power.

If someone takes the time and effort to express a perspective, it is our responsibility to listen for the core of what they are saying—whatever their pronunciation, enunciation, or word choice. To make sure we understand what they are actually communicating. To give them grace in case the idea doesn't come out fully formed and perfect, but to collectively work to understand what it is that matters to them—so much that they would take the risk to try to communicate the thought.

As much as we place the onus on the speaker to speak clearly and communicate effectively, we also need to challenge our own notions of effective communication. If we're only able to listen to people who look and sound like us, we're silencing people who communicate in any other way.

If we need to wait until we can all meet the standard of being well rested, well nourished, and supposedly clearheaded before we can use our voices, we're dismissing and discounting voices that don't have the systemic advantage to be in that life situation. We're only going to hear the voices of the people who have the power and privilege to speak.

Lower the stakes for someone by clearing out the assumption that our expression needs to be perfect according to one standard before we can use our voices.

How can we do this?

Recognize your defaults. What are your preferred communication styles and mediums? Which styles and mediums make it harder for you to metabolize information? Like with my friend, understand what mediums might make it easier for the other person to communicate. We don't all have to use the same modes, but we do need to figure out how to hear each other.

Articulate the norms in the relationship. Whether in a team setting or personal relationship, saying, "I'd love to hear what you're thinking, even if it's not fully formed, and even if you don't feel as coherent as you'd like to be, or "Emotions are welcome; we're humans, not robots," lowers the stakes and invites people in with more of their humanity.

Provide your endorsement of how someone communicates. You can invite people to listen to someone who isn't communicating in their preferred ways by saying, "I've asked Kiara to share today because she has the most nuanced take on this topic I've ever heard." Provide your reasoning for why you've invited the person so you use the social capital you have to get others to listen.

## Make Norms and Assumptions Explicit

In a season 6 episode of the TV show *Queer Eye*, Terri, a honky-tonk dance instructor known for her short shorts, and Ashley, her responsible adult daughter, have a fraught relationship. When Ashley has shared how she's feeling, Terri shuts down and is unable to make eye contact. Ashley feels like her mom isn't listening and feels even more isolated. As the show's resident relations expert, Karamo Brown unpacks the relationship. Viewers come to learn that when Ashley shares, Terri feels judged and ashamed, which is why she can't respond in the moment. But Terri promises that she always goes home and thinks about what Ashley has said for days.

In the end, Terri and Ashley agree on a code word that helps them get what they need and affirms the relationship. When Terri feels overwhelmed and needs more time to process, she'll say "Karamo!" And when Ashley feels like her mother isn't listening and she needs more connection, she'll say "Karamo!" The common understanding of how they communicate differently, along with the clear norm of what to do if they feel stuck, helps them move forward together.

Understanding and renegotiating the norms of how we communicate allows each of us to better use our voices. Unspoken norms silence those who don't know what the norms are or means they have to figure them out by trial and error over time. Clear and discussable norms help us know where, when, and how voice is welcome.

Whether in relationship, work, or community, most of us want to follow the rules. In order to do so, we need to know what the rules are—and how they are changing as each of us evolves in our own process of unlearning silence and appreciating voice. Dominant norms seem obvious to those with dominant identities but are often opaque to those with subordinated identities. We can stay more in sync and aid each other in this journey by making explicit the norms that often remain unspoken. We can eliminate the guesswork, and its possible consequences, when we make norms discussable.

At work, making these norms explicit means articulating what you otherwise assume to be normal or obvious. If you have a comment, should you wait to be invited into the conversation or just say what you think when you think appropriate? If someone says something, is the idea final or just an idea? If there's an issue, are you assuming people will proactively raise it?

Setting these norms at the beginning of a new team project or in an existing relationship takes no more than thirty seconds, but can save hours of headache and weeks of frustration.

As strange as it might feel, having these conversations also helps our personal relationships by minimizing miscommunication and getting clear on how we can support one another. If there's something to discuss, does it work for us to text about it or to save it for our next family meeting? If I'm on the fence about whether I can really make the girls' trip, is it better for me to tell you now or cancel at the last minute? Simple statements like "It's been a long week. Can we promise not to take offense if I fall asleep while we're watching the movie?" and "I love you. I'm not in the habit of saying it, but I don't ever want you to doubt my care for you" can stave off painful misunderstanding.

Part of making norms explicit is also acknowledging when the norms have evolved.

Leanna loved traveling with her girlfriends, even though she wished their plans didn't always have to be so rigid. While Leanna had always been game to chase adventure, Celeste liked plans and predictability. Celeste was the one who organized their plans in color-coordinated spreadsheets—yellow for transportation, green for outdoor activities, purple for meals, orange for individual choice, red for emergency contacts—and settled the group bills. As annoying as Celeste's rules could be, everyone also knew that she was the one who made the trips happen.

After the first few trips together, Celeste had everyone trained. If your checked bag was overweight, you'd never live it down. If you showed up at the appointed time, it was considered late. If you showed up late, you had to buy everyone dinner. If you were going somewhere and didn't tell someone, she really would call the authorities.

As Leanna packed for this year's trip, she felt the tension start to build in her shoulders. She loved her girlfriends. Time with them was worth it, she told herself. Even if she could do without some of Celeste's uptightness. She heard Celeste's mantra in her head—leave enough time to get to the airport, enough time in case you hit traffic, enough time for the unexpected. Leanna set her alarm clock for 3:45 a.m.

At the airport, Leanna and her friends looked at each other. As happy as they were to see each other, they were confused. Where was Celeste? They'd texted her. She would never be late. Had she gotten hit by a bus while on her way?

A few minutes later, Celeste strolled in with bags in tow.

"Who *are* you?" Leanna blurted to Celeste.

"What? That's the hello I get?" replied Celeste with a smile.

Leanna couldn't believe it. The rules that they had fought over for so many years had changed without so much as a word? While she was all for a more relaxed Celeste, had she known that showing up at the scheduled time was no longer considered late, she would have slept in and done her hair.

"Can't a girl change?" quipped Celeste.

"Of course. But let us know so the rest of us aren't sitting around waiting for *you*."

People can change and norms can evolve, and it helps everyone to make the norms clear.

## TACTICAL WAYS TO SUPPORT VOICE

While I've chosen to focus this chapter on several of the main ways we can stop unintentionally silencing people, there are plenty of other ways we silence those around us. Below is a nonexhaustive list of actions that help support voice. Use the checklist below to see which you regularly do and which you might add to your mix.

- *Attribute ideas correctly.* Who actually came up with the idea? Give credit where due. (For more on this, see chapter 10.)
- *Don't talk over other people.* Let people finish their thoughts before adding your own. If you interrupt someone, apologize and invite them to finish their thought.
- *Create opportunities.* Where can someone else (not you) take the lead? Delegate authority and make clear you are inviting them to do things their own way.
- *Publicly endorse their ideas.* Amplify someone else's voice by offering your public support of them. Private encouragement is nice, but public support puts your social capital behind their voice.

> • *Give people a platform.* Are there clear spaces where people
> can take the stage and share their thoughts? If you have a
> platform, can someone guest post so your listeners or
> followers hear them?
>
> Which of these actions are second nature to you? More
> important, which of these would the people around you say
> you actively and regularly do? Which of these do you need to
> reincorporate into your daily practice until they become a
> habit?

## Get Out of the Way

Roberto was the founder of a successful community organization
focused on eradicating food insecurity. He was well respected by everyone. His ability to humanize the effort and tap into networks was
unparalleled.

He also realized that whenever he was in the room, people would
defer to him. Even when he said he didn't have a specific opinion,
that he was just there to lend support and that he would defer to
whoever the decision maker was, people still looked to him. When
Roberto showed up at a team meeting, lighthearted banter and generative conversation would stop. Everyone looked to him. A hush
came over the room. "This sounds like a great conversation and
meeting. Please don't let me get in the way," Roberto would say.

As much as he tried to make his presence invisible, just being in
the room silenced others. When Roberto noticed this pattern, he
stopped going to the team meetings. Not showing up was the way he

could best support the voices of the people he and the organization needed to hear from.

Where do we need to *not* be present in order to support and unleash other voices? Where does our presence—or the shadow of our influence—dim the work of others?

Sometimes, the best way to support someone else's voice is to get out of the way.

OUR INTENTIONS ARE ONLY AS GOOD AS THEIR IMPACT.

Now that we're more aware of the ways we unintentionally silence people and know what to do instead, we can choose to do better. We can influence other people's decisions to choose silence or choose voice by listening, clearing preconceived notions, centering their interests and agency, normalizing different styles of communication, making norms explicit, and getting out of the way.

While our individual actions and interpersonal efforts have a profound impact on whether people are silenced, voice also requires systemic change. Change is most powerful when we "do the work" individually (which the majority of this book has covered) and pair that with systemic and policy changes. In the next chapter, we'll explore ways to unlearn systemic silence so that the systems around us better support voice.

# YOUR TURN

## Reflect

Which of these strategies for supporting voice might you try to implement? Where, when, and with whom?

What preconceived notions do you hold about certain people or groups of people?

What norms and assumptions might you need to make explicit?

## Experiment

Practice listening across difference.

- The next time you find yourself in a conversation with someone expressing a perspective different from your own, explicitly adopt the experimentation stance.

- Depending on your relationship with them, you might even be transparent and say, "I'm really working on listening across differences. So I'm going to be trying to listen to understand, even as right now I see things differently."

As you listen, look for answers to these questions:

- What are they really trying to say?

- What do they want me to do?

- Why do they think that is a good course of action?

    Bonus: build your capacity to hear different voices
    by reading books, listening to podcasts, or consuming
    media by people who have different communication
    styles, politics, and perspectives than you do.

In a situation where you feel the need to step in, ask:

- Is this about me or about them?

- Do I know (from them) what would most support them?

- How can I act in solidarity with the cause?

# 10

# Change the System

As schools shut down for the first COVID lockdown in March 2020, I found myself wandering the neighborhood with a toddler in tow, trying to burn off the energy that otherwise had him literally bouncing off the walls. I wasn't alone. We were taking our "adventure walks" with seemingly every other mother in the neighborhood. Not because these moms didn't have finely honed expertise and impactful careers. Not because we didn't have supportive spouses. Not because we hadn't been raised to believe that we could be anything we wanted to be.

But because it made sense, given the circumstances, for us to be the ones caring for children during the day and sneaking work in during the night. It made sense for my spouse—the person with the salaried job, to which the family's health insurance was attached—to work during the prime hours to keep his job. Of course it made sense for me, the family member who was more used to and therefore more able to multitask, context-switch, and juggle, to do just that.

I write this fully aware of the privilege of having flexible work and a two-parent household that allowed me to care for our child during the day. But the circumstances that led to more women shouldering childcare responsibilities than men at that time was not by accident.

As I commiserated with other moms about losing decades of progress on gender equity in the span of a few days, we also realized something important. The solution didn't exist in any of our families alone. Our lives were inextricably shaped by the factors around us.

Whether it is a family, organization, or social group, each system purposefully elevates certain voices and silences others. For there to be greater gender equity in my family and marriage, there needs to be universal health care, childcare, leave policies—and the list goes on. For each of us to find, hone, and use our voices, we need the systems around us not to silence us. And for each of us to learn how not to silence others, we need the systems around us to support voice rather than silence.

Having a seat at the table.

Being in the right rooms.

Being valued for what you bring.

Having power and influence.

None of this happens by accident. They are the result of the systems we create and perpetuate.

Writing this chapter feels daunting, because changing existing systems can be daunting. How are any of us supposed to change systems that have existed for centuries? How are we supposed to change the system when other people who have more power have active incentives to maintain the status quo? After all, the current billionaires of the world don't need the system to change. The system seems to be working just fine for them.

Systemic change is slow and costly. The cards can feel stacked against us. But these systems haven't always been here, no matter how timeless and entrenched they may seem. Whether it's capitalism, patriarchy, or systemic racism, these are systems people have created, and that we *can* change.

In this chapter, I'll outline the two biggest culprits of systemic silence: policies and practices. I'll analyze five concrete things we can do in everyday life that help us unlearn systemic silence. And I'll offer questions for you to answer about the systems you may be affected by, and benefit from, so you can lend your voice to systemic change as you choose.

## What Is a System, Anyway?

A system is a series of policies and practices that shape those who live within it. Try as we might, none of us live in isolation from one another. Systems thinking acknowledges that all the pieces of a family, organization, or society impact one another.[1]

Created by psychiatrist Murray Bowen in the late 1940s, family systems theory argues that people cannot be understood in isolation from one another. The relationship our parents have (or don't have) with each other and the relationships we have (or don't have) with our parents and siblings all impact how we interact with people.[2] Even if we sever ties with our family of origin, we still take all the baggage from our family system into the new family systems we enter. Whether it is a work family, chosen family, or what-did-I-marry-into family, if we are in relationship with other people, we are part of a relationship system.

As much power and opportunity as there is in unlearning interpersonal silence, we cannot deny the impact that systems have on each of us. Systems are what reinforce our inclination toward voice or silence. Unlearning silence requires understanding the patterns of silence in the systems we're part of and figuring out how we can change them to better support voice.

## What Impact Does a Policy Have?

Kate was thrilled to get a job. She had been out of work for fourteen months. Unemployment checks had long stopped coming. Her credit cards were maxed out, and having a steady income was the relief that she had been looking for. After 3,478 job applications, countless networking calls, 23 job interviews, and 4 final rounds, a job was finally hers.

So when her employer sent through a nondisclosure agreement (NDA) as part of the standard employment contract, Kate didn't think twice before signing it. After all, who was she to negotiate? She was optimistic about this company being a good fit. The agreements were standard in the industry. Mostly, she needed a paycheck again.

A few months into the job, Kate went to HR to share her concerns about how work was being allocated. It seemed like she was getting the short end of the stick when it came to assignments and brutal on-call hours. Sure, she was the most junior, but the standards seemed different for her than for others on the team.

Then word came that the company did not think she was a fit. She was going to be let go. After all, she was an at-will employee.

Her friends told her to sue the company for wrongful termination. They couldn't just fire her. She should expose how they treated her. Make it go viral.

Kate went back and read the paperwork. There it was—her signature on the mandatory arbitration and mutual nondisclosure agreement. Kate had indeed agreed that she would not "directly or indirectly,

make, publish, or communicate any defamatory or disparaging remarks, comments, or statements concerning the Company or any of
its employees, officers, shareholders, members . . ." Her heart sank.

In each system, there are rules that supposedly govern it. We'll
call those rules policies. And then there is how the rules actually
play out. We'll call those practices. The rule is that kids are not supposed to talk back—that's the policy. But it's okay for your younger
brother to because he's the favorite child—that's the practice. Both
the policies and practices within a system reinforce how a system
works—and have the potential to change it.

Policies like nondisclosure and nondisparagement clauses are
designed to silence. The power differentials between employers and
employees, particularly in Kate's situation, are stark. Fear of losing
the offer means that individual employees are unlikely to negotiate
the terms. If you want the job, you have to sign the paperwork. The
power sits with the company.

If you change the policy, then you change the power dynamics. If
you change the policy, you can change the system.

Why do NDAs exist in the first place? The NDA was originally
intended to protect trade secrets from going from one organization
to a competitor. They became standard because broad nondisclosure benefits the company drafting the agreements. But NDAs also
silence workers during employment and confine them to their current job.[3] NDAs that trade financial settlement for silence mean
that the practices that triggered the complaints often remain unad-
dressed. Even if the enforceability of such agreements is hotly contested based on jurisdiction, the existence of the agreement itself
has a chilling effect. For one person to challenge the enforceability
of the agreement comes at huge personal cost to that individual. It
makes sense why any one individual would take a payout or simply

walk away and try to move on with their lives. Changing the default
policy means that the burden of enforced silence wouldn't fall on
any one individual.

Confidentiality makes sense for trade secrets. But if you're treating people well, confidentiality shouldn't be necessary for how you
treat people. If you have nothing to hide, why would you require silence?

An NDA is only one example of a policy that inclines people toward silence. Consider:

Requiring job applicants to have a college degree.

Tying compensation to years of prior experience rather than
ability.

Not providing paid family leave.

Each policy has the effect of editing out—or silencing—a segment
of the population.

When Karina's company was debating whether to offer parental
leave as part of their benefits package, her colleague joked, "We
should just not hire women of child-rearing age."

The thing about humor is that there's always an element of painful truth. Karina quickly put a stop to that thinking.

To set the record straight, it is illegal to discriminate against
candidates based on life situation. Second, those protections exist in
policy because family leave is expensive. As much as Karina hated
that her colleague could joke about it, she also understood where
they were coming from. Offering paid family leave when the country
or state doesn't provide it is a significant commitment for an organization. If looking only at the financial bottom line, offering paid
family leave doesn't make sense. It may not be financially tenable for
small businesses. But if we care about parents being able to do
meaningful work and believe that motherhood shouldn't mean that

you can't contribute meaningfully to society outside of the home, then we should offer a leave policy—even if that means reduced short-term profit. In a perfect world, the government would offer paid family leave. But when it doesn't, the policy choices we make as business owners have the net impact of silencing a group of people by forcing them to make the impossible (and unnecessary) choice between work and family.

Policies have the power to exclude—and therefore silence—groups of people.

In many cases the policies are doing what those in power intend them to do—protect the company and maintain the power of those who already hold power. But if that's not the intent of the policy, or if the policy is having an impact we don't intend, how might we rally to change it?

When we look at policies in an organization or even at home, we can do a systemic silence policy audit. Look at who the policies protect and whose voices they center and silence. Question why the policies exist, and how you might be able to achieve the same intended outcome (for example, protecting trade secrets) without the additional breadth that impacts others' dignity. In examining the policies in your system, interrogate:

What is the policy actually trying to achieve?

How does this policy silence people?

If we are committed to voice, how might we need to change the policy?

Are the policies having the impact you intend and supporting the culture that you want to build in your family, on your team, in your organization or country? If not, change the policy. If you're not the policy or decision maker, who is? How can you influence that person or group of people to reconsider the policy? What policy would better serve the needs of the group? Just because the policy has existed doesn't mean it needs to continue to exist.

## What Impact Does a Practice Have?

Calvin looked at the website for days before getting the nerve to show up at a local running group. Having embraced his "dad bod" in the years leading up to his divorce, he was afraid that he would be too slow, that he wasn't hard-core enough, and that he would be left behind. But this running group promised to be different. In bright orange typeface on every page of the website was the slogan: No one runs alone.

The first time, Calvin didn't run alone. He was with a group of cheerful, welcoming runners. On the way home, he exhaled with relief that this group was different.

But over time, he realized that he was running alone. He would start with a group, but the other runners would speed up and leave him behind without even realizing it. When he mentioned it to the leaders of the group, they told him it couldn't be happening. He just needed to join a different pace group. Yet week after week, he was left to run alone. Eventually, Calvin quit. If he was going to run alone, he didn't have to get up early and drive across town to do it.

What we put into practice—whether it's in a community running group, as a family, as coworkers, or even as a society—can foster belonging, preserve dignity, and move toward justice. These shared practices can become shared values, which help a system work cohesively, especially as it expands. Or these values and practices can become empty promises.

Policies are only as good as their practice.

We can incentivize voice within and across systems by making the implicit rules explicit, creating clear avenues for people to speak up, and insisting that unlearning silence is essential.

## Make the implicit rules explicit

It hadn't occurred to Kate to negotiate the terms of the employment contract.

At the time, she was just so grateful to have an offer letter in hand. It wasn't clear that any of the terms were negotiable, and not knowing what the rules were, Kate didn't want to risk the offer.

Women have historically been less likely than men to negotiate, unless explicitly told that negotiating is permitted.[4] In a study of MBA students, researchers found that about half of men negotiated their job offers, while only 12 percent of women negotiated theirs.[5]

And with good reason. Studies show that the social cost of negotiating is insignificant for men, but significant for women.[6] When women negotiate, people are more likely to see them as difficult and are less inclined to want to work with them and turn them down more often.[7]

Given that women stand to lose more than a million dollars in salary over a lifetime by not negotiating their original starting salary, being explicit that negotiation is okay or expected matters.[8]

The ambiguity of the rule silences those not in the know. Most of us want to follow the rules, we just don't always know what they are. As we discussed in chapter 3, when rules aren't clear, silence is more likely to make sense because the onus is on the individual to test the waters and incur the cost of getting the rules wrong. Putting the onus on the individual to negotiate a package effectively silences them.

Making implicit rules explicit forces us to reckon with the rules to see whether we're really living as we intend. It sheds light on the places where there's disconnect between our intent, our policies, and our practices. If the intent is to hire good talent, level the playing field, and create sustainable employment arrangements, making clear what is and isn't negotiable is a way to save everyone energy. Better yet, publish meaningful salary ranges to reduce information asymmetry.

So why don't people make rules explicit more often? Because demystifying the rules removes the structural advantage previously given to people who were in the know—the old boys' club and the sorority sisters. Because saying that you're open to negotiation means the company might end up paying more. Because making rules explicit forces us to reckon with the policies and practices we're actually living by. Because explicit rules put a stake in the ground, which people can push back on when they see practices that don't align.

If information is power, sharing information is a way of redistributing power that results in greater voice. In any system, the amount of time, energy, and effort spent deciphering what the rules really are systematically silences those who aren't already in the know.

## Create clear avenues for speaking up

I was recently working with a mission-driven organization that scaled quickly from a local team of 12 to over 150 employees around the world. The founders of the organization had been successful in part because of their feedback-rich culture. I was brought in to help with a challenge—to maintain that level of feedback at scale.

Back in the day you just walked down the hall to a founder's office and had a conversation. Now, if an employee wants to give feedback, what are they supposed to do? With a company of this size, what's the avenue to offer thoughts without the message just going into the void?

The lack of clarity about where to go and what to do is yet another hurdle that silences us when we most need to use our voices. It is hard enough—particularly in moments of crisis or trauma—to think about saying something, much less have to figure out the mechanics of where, how, and to whom I share the thoughts.

A good example of making the avenues clear is the NotMe app.[9] The platform provides end-to-end whistleblowing, investigation, and case management software for organizations. It provides the option for people to report concerns anonymously, while maintaining the possibility of conversation in order to better understand the issue. Most important, the software design lowers the barrier for reporting misconduct by offering sample language for describing the behavior you're reporting. Reporting harassment is never easy, but clicking "inappropriate jokes" or "expressions of sexual interest" and categorizing the behavior as physical, verbal, or financial with the click of a button is far easier than trying to come up with the language itself. And if there is an area of concern, the tool provides a clear pathway for communicating those concerns and ensuring that the issue is investigated in a systematic way.

The NotMe app is a great example of how clear avenues with transparent norms and suggested language support voice. It's not unlike how swiping left to reject someone on a dating app is a lot easier than telling someone directly to their face that you would never date them.

Having clarity about how someone can share what matters to them takes the guesswork out of our most treasured relationships.

Mila was worried about her dad. He had been searching for love for most of Mila's adult life. In her opinion, he was a bit too desperate. She fretted that his unyielding desire to be in a relationship clouded his judgment.

Then came Hannah. Hannah was a far cry from what Mila would have wanted for her dad, but he glowed in her presence. As happy as Mila was that he was happy, *There's no way she can really be into him. She's way out of his league*, Mila thought.

Mila's suspicions intensified when she overhead Hannah disparage her dad to someone on the phone when she thought no one else was home. Mila wanted to say something, but it seemed like there was never an opportunity for her to speak privately with her dad. Hannah was always around when Mila visited him.

Unfortunately, Mila's fears were confirmed. Hannah disappeared— but not before draining his savings account and buying a new car. When Mila finally mentioned to her dad that she'd known Hannah wasn't good for him, her dad asked, "Why didn't you tell me?"

Mila responded, "You were so happy. And there was never a moment when it was just the two of us. I didn't know if you'd believe me."

And only then did the avenue become clear. Her dad said, "If there's something you need to say, text me. I always want to know."

Life is full of difficult thoughts to share and challenging conversations to have, especially with those close to us. Knowing where, when, and how to start a difficult conversation reduces barriers to having it at all.

## Make unlearning silence a competency

Tanisha was stunned. After being in counseling for months with her husband, Eliot, he shared a story that explained so much. "I used to hide my homework and throw it out," he explained. "I didn't need or want my parents to see it because they would always have something mean to say."

That single anecdote explained the tension that had been growing in their relationship. Tanisha was fast to fix things and offer feedback, when all Eliot wanted to do was hide his work to avoid that exact outcome.

Leaving their therapist's office, Tanisha decided to say something. "I hadn't heard that story before. I'm not mad or angry or anything—just sort of surprised that you hadn't mentioned something so big earlier."

Eliot turned to his wife of ten years and said, "I didn't want to be a burden. I assumed you didn't want or need to know."

"But now that I do, I totally understand where you're coming from. I can see how we're affecting each other and how we might change the way we're interacting so that we can support one another better," Tanisha explained. "Would you be open to sharing more about how you feel and think with me?"

If we value the intimacy of relationship and the dignity of being known, unlearning silence is not only a journey for ourselves, but needs to be a shared personal value and norm in our families, friendships, and partnerships.

If organizations are serious about creating spaces where innovation, collaboration, diversity, equity, inclusion, and belonging are realities, unlearning silence needs to be a leadership competency. Specifically, unlearning the ways we silence those around us.

Providing emotional support as a matter of crisis management can no longer be relegated to office housework that women (particularly of color) volunteer for or are assigned simply because of the identities they hold.

Creating psychological safety on a team and listening across differences are not optional soft skills. They are the human-centered, interpersonal skills that should differentiate those we promote. Naming these skills as core competencies and using them as bases for promotion sends the message that we actually value these skills.

These skills are prerequisites for promotion. What gets rewarded gets repeated.

Which also means that regardless of how technically savvy Jared in IT is or how much revenue Scott brings in, if they don't also demonstrate the abilities to listen across differences, create psychological safety, and support others' voices, they will not be rewarded. Building a culture of voice rather than silence requires leaders within the system to lead and be rewarded for these skills.

## What Can I Do?

If you're seeking tangible actions you can take that will change the system, this next section is for you. I'll outline five things we can do that can't help but impact the systems we're part of—even if we're not the policymakers.

### Embrace your power

When we feel trapped by the system, it is easy to think that we have no power. The system feels like Goliath, and we're David without any stones to throw.

I'm just a cog in a wheel.

I'm the middle child, and we always get the short end of the stick.

Nothing I do or say matters anyway.

Or so we come to believe. And that's what systems and the people who benefit from them want us to believe. But that's not true. Power is the ability to influence others. We each hold power.

Social psychologists John French and Bertram Raven identified five bases of power in 1959, with Raven adding the sixth in 1965.[10]

1. **Legitimate:** *Power based on hierarchy or official role.* A prime minister has power because they currently hold the office.

2. **Reward:** *Power to give or withhold rewards.* Customers can write positive or negative restaurant reviews online.

3. **Expert:** *Power based on specific knowledge or skill.* As a physician-scientist and immunologist, Dr. Anthony Fauci knows more about infectious disease than most.

4. **Referent:** *Power based on how much people like and want to be like you.* Every influencer ever.

5. **Coercive:** *Power to penalize others.* Children screaming bloody murder during long car rides.

6. **Information:** *Power based on information you have.* People who were actually at the scene of a crime.

The different types of power remind me that while we may not feel powerful, we each have power. In a corporation, it can feel like all the power is at the top. After all, the C-suite holds legitimate power to make decisions that impact everyone. They also have the power to either give or withhold rewards in the form of bonuses, merit increases, and promotions, as well as coercive power to give poor performance reviews or put word out that you're difficult to work with.

Ofra, a graduate assistant intern at the same company, feels powerless. Sure, Ofra doesn't have as much legitimate or reward power as those in the C-suite. But as one of the only people who actually knows where the extra centrifuges are in the lab, Ofra has both expert and information power to make or break an experiment. As an intern with firsthand experience within the company, Ofra has power to either reward or punish the company with the way she describes her experiences in a Glassdoor review and to other students on campus trying to figure out whether the company is an employer of choice. As the only person of color working at a company that has set diversity goals, Ofra inherently holds the coercive power to make or break those goals.

Not everyone holds each type of power, but we each hold some power. Consider what types of power you hold in each of the systems you're in. If people like and want to be like you, you hold referent power. If you have a specific skill or set of knowledge, you have expert power. With social media and cancel culture, most of us have more coercive power than we used to. That's why you often get a faster reply tagging a company on social media rather than calling their customer service department.

Once we acknowledge what power we have, the next question becomes clear.

How can we use the power we have rather than focusing on what we don't have?

For years, families of prisoners of war were advised to stay silent. Under the "Keep Quiet" rule, family members were instructed not to say anything about their loved ones being captured. The argument went that if families said something, the prisoners might be badly treated or executed.[11] The idea was that any media coverage would complicate efforts to get their loved ones home.[12]

However, wives of POWs in Vietnam discovered that using media was actually more effective in getting their husbands home, because media raised awareness of the human rights violations taking place.[13] The wives defied the idea that legitimate power (through diplomacy) was the only way to bring their loved ones home.

What power do you have?

How can you use that power for the causes you care about within your family, company, and community?

## Choose voice

If silence breeds silence, voice can also breed voice.

The more we share our stories, the more our stories can encourage and inspire others and normalize the topics and challenges we're talking about. Not everyone has the privilege of being able to share with little consequence. But when we have the ability to weather the criticism and blowback that might come, sharing our stories paves the way for normalizing the issue of concern.

Let's take mental health. Stigma, prejudice, and discrimination attached to mental illness have long interfered with people seeking help, treatment, and recovery. The more people stayed silent about their own mental health challenges, the more stigmatized the challenges were. Thankfully a recent study evaluating changes in mental illness stigma in the United States over the course of twenty-two years shows that there is less stigma around depression now than there was twenty years ago.[14]

Younger generations are less likely to distance themselves from people with depression in social, professional, and family situations.[15] Millennials are twice as likely as baby boomers to be comfortable discussing mental health,[16] which is important because knowing or having contact with someone with mental illness is one of the best ways to reduce stigma. In 1996, 57 percent of Americans were not willing to have someone with depression marry into their family. In 2018, the number dropped to 40 percent. It means it's easier to talk about depression without fear of people distancing themselves from you.

From Lady Gaga to Dwayne "The Rock" Johnson, celebrities sharing their stories about mental health challenges brings the discussion into the mainstream. It has also reshaped the perception of whether success and mental health challenges can coexist. Spoiler: they can.

We've shifted from mental health not being something that people talked about to mental health being part of mainstream conversation. In many contexts, saying "I've got therapy" or "I was talking with my therapist" is now about as common as talking about what you had for lunch. Because more folks are talking about mental health, the challenges are increasingly normalized and seen as part of general health rather than something about which to keep silent.

From mental health to sexual orientation to miscarriages to racism to harassment, the systemic shift to normalize, decrease stigma, and increase access to resources starts with more open conversation.

Personally, I've been shocked at how often sharing one's story leads someone else to say, "Me too." Those two words can make the challenges visible, which is the first step to making them addressable. Change truly can begin by saying to someone, "Hey, I'm struggling with . . . ," or being open to hearing that from someone else.

Unlearning silence means challenging the social notions of what is acceptable, what needs to be swept under the rug, and what we choose to acknowledge as real. Ask yourself, Who does my silence protect? Are those the people and systems I want to protect? If not, that's one weight to tip the scale toward choosing voice.

Whatever the topic, sharing your story only seems strange because it hasn't been done before. But "weird" and "different" are at the heart of innovation and choosing a new way forward. How will you use your voice to encourage voice?

## Form coalitions

As a non–sports fan, I've been struck by the loyalty people have to sports teams. Yet living in the San Francisco Bay Area means that the Golden State Warriors have become my basketball team. In the mid-2010s, Warriors head coach Steve Kerr introduced a phrase that became the Warriors' slogan—"Strength in Numbers."[17] The phrase wasn't just a marketing slogan, but a mindset. Everyone has a different role to play.

Prior to winning the NBA championship in 2015, the Warriors' last championship win came by defeating the Washington Bullets 4–0 in the 1974–75 season.[18] After a forty-year dry spell, the team made it to the championships six times between 2015 and 2022, winning four titles in eight years with one of the strongest and deepest benches in the world.

In what came to be known as the "dynastic core," Andre Iguodala brought versatility. Klay Thompson shot and changed speed. Draymond Green brought fire and competitiveness. Stephen Curry made seemingly effortless half-court three-pointers and provided intentional leadership.

And it's not just the players on the roster. It's known that the Warriors' home arena is the hardest place for a visiting team in the NBA to win because of the strength of the fans. The players thrive on the energy, and the solidarity supercharges the home team to victory.[19]

Systemic change can start with but cannot be achieved by one person alone. We know that social isolation leads to adverse outcomes including depression, poor sleep, loss of executive function, and accelerated cognitive decline.[20] We know that workplace isolation reduces creativity, erodes performance, enhances turnover, and leads to emotional exhaustion.[21] In contrast, coalitions—a joining of forces and resources for a specific purpose—can catalyze change that wouldn't be possible separately.[22] Political coalitions form not because everyone's interests are completely aligned, but because the reality is that we can get more done together than apart.

Anytime we're less than 15 percent of the majority dominant group, we're easily tokenized—dismissed as weird or other.[23] If less than 15 percent of the total, we're highly watched, isolated from social settings where trust and relationship are built, and feel pressure to assimilate to the group norms.[24] Building a coalition reduces social isolation, opens the opportunity for belonging, and gets us over the 15 percent threshold.

It is common practice for people with subordinated identities to connect with other people with subordinated identities before going into a meeting, so that you know at least someone has your back. Rather than having to correct someone when they inevitably mispronounce your name, the other person can pronounce your name correctly when they reference you. We socialize ideas before taking them to leadership, so you know that you have a certain amount of support before putting yourself out there. We consult with other friends in our friend group before deciding which two of us should warn our girlfriend that her boyfriend is seeing other women. As exhausting as these practices might sound, the informal coalition means that you're using the cards you have and not going it alone.

As you look around, think about who else might share or be sympathetic to your concerns? Where might you be able to work together for a common goal? By sharing the ball and working together, the Warriors defied the well-worn model that a successful basketball team had to hinge around a single Michael Jordan– or LeBron James–type superstar. The Warriors are more powerful together. We are more powerful together.

## Attribute work accurately

People love a hero story. We want to believe that a single person can slay dragons, overcome evil, and win. The focus on a single hero makes for good superhero movies but effectively silences the contributions of the many.

If you're someone with subordinated identities, having your idea co-opted and passed off as their own by someone else with dominant identities is an experience all too familiar, but nonetheless infuriating. Female staffers in the Obama administration famously adopted a strategy of amplification—when a woman makes a key point, other women would repeat the point and give credit to the author. The practice forced men in the room to recognize the contribution and prevented them from claiming the idea as their own.[25]

Media has a habit of featuring the individual and erasing the team. When *Forbes* introduced the world's youngest billionaires in 2022, the cover photo featured three White men—suggesting that the youngest billionaires, or most worthwhile billionaires, were all

White men. However, in reality, twelve people had achieved the status, and four were Asian and two were women.[26] Similarly, when *The Globe and Mail* in the UK celebrated a venture capital firm co-led by partners Boris Wertz and Angela Tran, the photo accompanying the article only featured Wertz.[27] While each of these instances might seem innocuous, the choice of who to feature exhibits bias toward White men and reinforces a false stereotype of who is successful.

This exclusionary pattern silences the real work—and wins—of women and people of color. And it doesn't just happen in the world of work outside the home. In the 1980s, sociologist Arlene Kaplan Daniels coined the term *invisible work* to describe forms of unpaid labor like housework and volunteer work that are integral to making society function but are culturally and economically devalued.[28]

Wandering the neighborhood with my son during lockdown, I often felt invisible—because I was spending a lot of my time performing this kind of invisible work. And I'm not alone. Globally, women perform three out of every four hours of unpaid labor.[29] Silent work fills in for the lack of social services and sustains economies. Unpaid care and domestic work is valued to be 10–39 percent of GDP and contributes more to the economy than manufacturing, commerce, or transportation sectors.[30]

If we stay silent about the work we do—at an office or in our homes—it remains invisible. By naming the work, we make it visible.

My friend who left her job at a pharmaceutical company to be a stay-at-home mom struggles with whether she's contributing enough to her family because she doesn't bring home a paycheck. In a frustrated moment, we quantified the financial value of the work she is doing. If she was not caring for their two children, they would need to hire a nanny or pay for day care, to the tune of $1,800 a month per child. There already, she is delivering $3,600 a month of value, or $42,000 a year. If she were not going grocery shopping, they would need to pay for a service to deliver the groceries. If she were not cleaning the house, they would be hiring a housekeeper. If she were not doing the yard work, they would need to hire a gardener. As we added up the numbers, we found that the work she was doing was bringing $80,000 of monetary value per year—more than her spouse's annual salary.

Giving credit where credit is due recognizes people's different contributions. We can't appreciate and value invisible work until we unlearn our refusal to acknowledge its existence. Until we unlearn our silence about it. We can't value what we don't acknowledge.

## Direct your dollars

Every holiday season, signs pop up in store windows encouraging people to shop local. Instead of ordering a mug online, purchase one made by a local artisan. Instead of expanding a corporation's profits, support the work and livelihood of someone in your own neighborhood.

To be honest, I struggle with this idea, because one-click ordering with free shipping that puts something on my doorstep—or ships it free across the country—is incredibly attractive. And buying something from a big chain store means less money out of my pocket now than I'd need to pay the independent shop around the corner that's trying to make rent, pay a living wage, and still make a profit. And I'm not the only one. Because my neighbors face the same decisions, most of the mom-and-pop stores that made our neighborhood so unique have been replaced with big-box stores. This is the dilemma we each face each time we make a purchase.

We all have the power to support or silence products, projects, and people with how we spend money. The market can seem like an impersonal system detached from each of us. Unless we're Elon Musk or Jeff Bezos, will any of our financial decisions really make an impact?

We can't talk about systems without acknowledging the role of economic power in our systems. Like it or not, money talks. Every single one of us, in our own small way, determines what is stocked on the grocery store shelves, which films get made, and whose voices get to be heard.

For years, Hollywood executives claimed that non-White stars couldn't carry a movie. They argued that without a White lead, a movie wouldn't sell. Instead of featuring diverse casts, Hollywood whitewashed characters and continued to make movies that featured White male leads—and that movie critics tended to find mediocre at best.

But the research shows the opposite. Movies with non-White casts can be financially lucrative. In fact, movies with racially diverse casts are more profitable than those with all-White casts.[31]

*Black Panther* grossed over $1.4 billion worldwide, making it one of the highest-grossing films of all time.[32] *Crazy Rich Asians* grossed over $238 million on a budget of $30 million, making it the highest-grossing romantic comedy of the decade.[33]

Each of these landmark films was possible because you and I showed up at the box office to support and express our hunger for films that tell our stories. Perhaps one day, the list of Hollywood movies with non-White leads won't be so short.

Telling a different story seems risky because it hasn't been done. But sticking with the same formula continues to silence those who have been systemically underestimated and disadvantaged. The pattern of underestimation isn't just in which movies get made, but also in which ventures get launched.

In 2021, only 2.4 percent of the $330 billion of venture capital invested in start-ups in the United States went to companies founded only by women; 15.6 percent of the capital went to teams with both female and male founders.[34] Start-ups with at least one Black founder received 1.2 percent of overall venture dollars invested in the U.S. in 2022.[35] If you're a venture capitalist, who you are likely to fund is clear. These outcomes exist not because the ideas of women and people of color are worse, but because folks with the funding haven't traditionally been willing to invest in what could be.

If you're an investor, who are you going to invest in?

If you're looking for a vendor, who are you going to hire?

If you're a consumer, who are you going to purchase from?

Money is influence. I have to remind myself that how I use money is more than just how much is left in my bank account at the end of the month. Because how I use and spend money influences which projects, people, voices, and communities succeed. However large or small, our purchasing power has the ability to support or silence someone else's livelihood and dreams.

IT'S EASY TO POINT OUR FINGERS AT SYSTEMS AND SAY THAT THEY are broken. After all, most systems are depersonalized, so no one person is solely responsible. Existing systems typically want us to forget that we have power, because embracing our power means that we can effect change. Our decisions to follow or challenge the policies and practices that make up systems can change the course of history. The flow-on effect of each of us choosing voice, forming coalitions, attributing work accurately, and directing our dollars is to fundamentally shape and reshape the systems around us—and to either silence or support people.

Unlearning silence requires shifts in mindsets, skill sets, and systems. Whether in a family or a community, systemic change starts with one person being willing to take action.

Let that person be you.

# YOUR TURN

---

## Reflect

What systems are you a part of?

What is your role within each of these systems?

Within a system, what are you choosing to talk about and not talk about?

What type of power do you hold that you might be underestimating?

How does your silence or voice impact the system you're in?

Remember: systems are our interconnectedness. Changing your own contribution changes the system.

## Experiment

What pattern or policy do you want to change?

Who can you invite to join your effort?

What are you currently silent about where you might instead choose voice?

# Conclusion

As someone who has long been silent and silenced, I know that unlearning silence is not an easy ask. This work can be deeply uncomfortable, often raises things that need to be explored in therapy (I'm not joking!), and requires us to deconstruct and reconstruct how we show up in our day-to-day lives.

But unlearning silence is also the way we find and use our voices to build the families, communities, and world that we want. A world in which you and the people around you—and the people who come after you—can thrive.

For those of you who, like me, have spent a lifetime carefully calculating your words and actions, I hope this book has shown you that you are not alone. You're not being ridiculous. You're not overreacting or too sensitive.

It wasn't you.

In the future, I hope the times and places where you choose silence are ones that benefit you, rather than being comfortable and convenient for those around you.

I hope that you are more empowered and equipped to use your voice. With each experiment you try, I hope you find your voice growing stronger and more powerful.

I hope you find yourself living more freely and more able to be the person you want to be—the person only you can be. Because behind the silence you learned is a strong, powerful voice that is singularly yours.

And we need you.

Let's speak and fight for what is good, right, and true.

Let's rebuild a world in which each human being, regardless of the family and factors into which we were born, has the opportunity to be seen, known, and heard for who we are and who we are becoming.

Where the loudest, proudest, and most privileged voice doesn't automatically prevail, but there is space—and the active creation of space—for difference.

Where belonging, dignity, and justice are realities not just for a privileged few, but for each and every human being.

Where in workplaces, we spend less time posturing, tiptoeing, and figuring out work-arounds.

Where in creating space and celebrating voice, we are able to fully unleash talent and receive the rewards that collaboration and innovation have long promised.

Where in community we can unlearn and relearn the fundamental lessons that shape how we show up in the world.

Where in our families—by birth or by choice—the sense of being deeply known and loved is possible because editing and censoring ourselves is no longer required.

Where there is space and grace for each of us to be ourselves—and to be accepted, respected, even celebrated.

This is the opportunity of unlearning how we silence others.

And the opportunity of unlearning our own silence.

I can't wait to hear your voice.

# Unlearning Silence
# Road Map

## Introduction

## AWARENESS

### 1. The Silence We Learned

*What Is Voice?*

How We Learn Silence

    On an individual level

    On a structural level

    On a social level

    On an intrapersonal level

### 2. The Problem with Silence

Silence Leads to Self-Doubt

Silence Infringes Dignity

Silence Erases Our Sense of Selfhood

Our perception

The Difference? Agency.

## 4. How We Silence Ourselves

*Is It Them or Is It You? Likely Both.*

We Assume Our Voices Don't Matter

We focus too much on others' expectations

We give in to peer pressure

We value sameness over uniqueness

We Self-Censor

We Mitigate Our Speech

We Never Speak in the First Place

## 5. How We Silence Others

We Underestimate the Challenge

We Say We Want Input When We Really Don't

Three buckets

We Control the Narrative

We Rely on Flawed Reflexes

We Focus on Ourselves

Time of day

Communication mediums

Processing styles

We Change the Topic to Ourselves

We Don't Believe Them

We Hold a Fixed Mindset

We Build Cultures of Silence

We All Silence Others—But We Don't Have To

# ACTION

## 6. Find Your Voice

Cultivate Awareness

Your voice is worthy and deserves to be heard

People are going to try to shape your voice

Judgment—of your voice and who you are—
is normal

Interrogate Our Voices

Challenge your own thinking

Give yourself permission

Experiment with Using Your Voice

Do small experiments

Make experiments time bound

Get comfortable with being uncomfortable

Invite Voices into the Mix

    Balance the inputs

    Have a sounding board

    Decide whose voices are essential

    Invite your own reflection

    Regularly recalibrate

# 7. Use Your Voice

Three Levers for Voice

Substance

    What aspects of the substance are my domain?

    What perspective do I bring?

Relationship

    Disrupt bias

    Cultivate emotional culture

Process

    Design intentionally

*Don't Leave Meetings to Chance*

    Suggest process moves that support your voice

    Be explicit about implicit norms

    Have standard questions

    Tend to procedural justice

## 8. How to Speak Up

Start with Why

Connect the Dots

Make the Ask Clear

Embrace Resistance

## 9. Stop Silencing People

Listen, Especially Across Difference

Clear Preconceived Notions

Center Their Interests and Agency

*How to Do Your Own Work*

Normalize Different Styles of Communication

    Recognize your defaults

    Articulate the norms in the relationship

    Provide your endorsement of how someone
    communicates

Make Norms and Assumptions Explicit

*Tactical Ways to Support Voice*

Get Out of the Way

# 10. Change the System

# Conclusion

# Let's Go Deeper—
# A Gift for Readers

Navigate your journey with
the *Unlearning Silence* Reader's Guide,
a resource for digging deeper and taking action.
Find this and other resources at:

www.elainelinhering.com/guide

To book Elaine to speak or work with your team, visit:

www.elainelinhering.com

# Acknowledgments

Writing a book takes a village. Without Meghan Stevenson and her team, this book would not exist. You were the first to say this idea was like gold at the bottom of the BART tracks. Thank you for knowing how to package my ideas so the publishing world could see their value and making this new chapter possible. Cheers to your success.

To my agent, Rachel Ekstrom Courage. The first time we met, you said you would advocate for this project more than I would myself. I remember thinking that wasn't possible. And yet it was. Thank you for fighting for me, centering my needs, and guiding me through this roller coaster of authorship with steadiness and grace.

It is a gift to work with people who are incredible at their craft. My editor, Meg Leder, is undoubtedly one of them. Thank you for loving this project enough to be the fussiest editor when it was most needed, and a coach, thought partner, and wise and warm sage at all other times. You even showed up constructive and effective in the worst of my stress-driven nightmares. The book is crisper, clearer, and more cohesive because of Anna Argenio's incisive edits. I am more hopeful for the global impact of unlearning silence because of your fierce and unwavering advocacy.

To the Penguin Life team, thank you for dreaming with me and being such a dream to work with. Thank you, Isabelle Alexander and Annika Karody, for all the work that can go unseen but is so essential and deeply appreciated. Lydia Hirt and Shelby Meizlik helped me dream bigger than I ever imagined of where unlearning silence might heal and make us all more whole. Patrick Nolan saw and believed in the long-term potential of this book to change lives and make the world more of the one we'd want to live in. Getting to cry with you all on our first Zoom call was a sign that I'd found the right team. Alison Rich, Stephanie Bowen, Rachael Perriello Henry, and Zehra Kayi, you provided direction when I was lost and light when it was dark. Thank you for nudging me into the worlds I needed to enter. Sabila Khan, your infectious enthusiasm and conviction that this was the book you needed twenty years ago buoyed me through the hardest parts of the process. Thank you for getting the message out in more languages than I could have ever imagined. Brian Tart, Kate Stark, Lindsay Prevette, Molly Fessenden, Julia Falkner, Tricia Conley, Katie Hurley, Madeline Rohlin, Daniel Lagin, Jane Cavolina, Dorothy Janick, Tracy Gardstein: you've all taught me just how amazing things can be when you dare to trust your gut.

Steve Troha and the Folio Literary team supported me as a first-time author. Kelly Yun dove in headfirst to make sure everything was well researched and fact-based. I'm still embarrassed but endlessly grateful you unearthed bacteria per square inch to settle Toiletgate. Siri Chilazi offered generous recommendations, unwavering support, and unparalleled solidarity. Jennifer Kem used her incomparable ability to strategize to help me visionize, always starting with what I really want in life. Sarah Paikai, you showed me not just what competency can do, but how transformative an effective mobilizer can be. Thank you both for having my back.

My colleagues at Triad Consulting Group: Sheila Heen and Doug Stone got me off the big law conveyor belt and made a different path possible. From Hershey's chocolate bars with almonds to Knicks Linsanity T-shirts, you've both taught me so much about empathy, humility, teaching, and learning. Debbie Goldstein leaned into leadership so the writing of this book could happen and challenges people toward good yeses with warmth and compassion. Julie Okada saw and championed what I brought to the world far earlier than I ever dared imagine.

Jessie McShane taught me that celebration is one of the great joys (and necessities) of life. Lily Lin kept us organized and helped me learn to say no (I'm on sabbatical). Brenda Gutierrez wisely pushed us to do better. Anh Tran was real from the get-go and blesses the world with her genius. Sarah Brooks used her voice and made *ally* a verb. Heather Sulejman has been in the trenches and Caroline Adler showed us what could be.

Thank you, Alonzo Emery, for the SOS calls to maintain sanity; I'm proud of how far we've come as a no-longer-so-new generation of practitioners crafting our best lives. Angelique Skoulas, thank you for understanding how much space different parts of life take up and believing me when it mattered most. Stevenson Carlebach, Michele Gravelle, Ann Garrido, Peter Hiddema, Stephan Sonnenberg, Stacy Lennon, Emily Epstein, Bob Bordone, Michael Moffitt—you are part of shaping the facilitator and educator I am today.

Jamie Woolf and Heidi Rosenfelder offered creative genius, deep care, and hiking recommendations. Susanna Cooper, Michal Kurlaender, Claudia Escobar, Deborah Travis, and the Wheelhouse team connected me to some of the most meaningful work, causes, and communities. To each client who got these ideas, even when you needed a moment because the phrase alone blew your mind. This book would not be without your having trusted me with the most gnarly and tender of challenges throughout the years.

In a world where leadership books by women of color don't yet come up first in Google searches, Ruchika Tulshayan and Deepa Purushothaman have led the way and modeled an abundance mindset. Thank you for connecting me to some of my most treasured sisters in the cause. We may have been the first, few, or the only, but that will no longer be the case. Pooja Lakshmin, Luvvie Ajayi Jones, Elaine Welteroth, Ijeoma Oluo, Kelly Richmond Pope, Aiko Bethea, Kim Crowder, Elizabeth Leiba—you inspire me by your words and how you show up. Thank you, Kathy Khang, for raising your voice, and in your graciousness to remind me that there is room—and need—for each of our voices.

Kwame Christian told me I had everything I needed to do all of this and it meant the world. Amal Masri, thank you for holding me, understanding the yuck, and being my kitchen table.

Rosie Yeung, Alice Chan, Jessica Chen, Tara Robertson, Phil Xiao, Paul Ladipo, Francine Parham, Sybil Stewart. Your presence on LI and in my life have been transformative. Grateful is an understatement to know we are shaping the world to honor our individual and collective dignity.

Writing isn't just about the craft, but about the heart. Thank you, Regina Chow Trammel, for helping me heal, and Angela Park for being a fierce advocate. You both are who I want to be when I grow up. Alice Chen, Cassindy Chao, Belinda Luu, and my Feisty Sisters, you offer the invaluable gifts of not having to explain myself and focusing on how we can support one another.

Minna Dubin managed my mom rage and powered each Cafenated Coffee writing session. Jackie Knapp reminded me to play. Cathy Swinford kept me sane and is an example that the hard work of excavation and surrender to God is always worth it. Work outside the home does not happen without reliable childcare; Mayra Dana and Emilia O'Toole created a nurturing environment and helped to raise our children with unparalleled love and care. Dhanya Lakshmi, Lisa Hook, Nicole Hosemann, Anne Mayoral, Alison Kosinski, Summer Chang—raising young ones through a pandemic is not something we wish on anyone, but if we had to do it, there's no one else I'd rather do it with.

To my Benetton crew. From climbing mountains during hailstorms to showing up to surprise one another at Target, thank you for showing me the power of cross-cultural and racial solidarity, asking the hard questions, and helping me live with eternal perspective. Dr. Jennifer J. Stuart is head cheerleader and fierce advocate, whose keen questions and poignant observations have always struck to the heart in the best ways. It is true that behind every sane woman is another woman sneak-texting at midnight. Audrie Wright, you are that person. Heather and Ben Kulp, your infinite patience, wry humor, and faithful friendship steady me. Elizabeth Eshleman, you've taught me to sing, cry, and embrace life. Ge, thank you for helping me learn to say when I'm hungry and trusting me more than I've ever trusted myself. Thank you, BWB, for cell phones, prayer, culinary curation, and reminding me to do me.

Mom and Dad, thank you for praying me through and being adamant that I would have a career. From freezer stashes of handmade jiaozi to Friday night sleepovers so I could get sleep, this book—and my life—would not be possible without you. Thank you for your sacrifice, for the things I'm aware of and those we've yet to speak or know. Our journey together has taught me the power and promise of being able to continue to learn, together. I'm proud to be your daughter. To the Minnesota Herings, your commitment to continued experimentation and humble service inspire me.

Laz, I'm honored to get to be your mother. Don't lose your curious confidence and clarity in who you are. Red garbage trucks with grabber arm hugs forever. M, thank you for having always loved and encouraged my voice, even before I really found it. ISTYPN.

Thank you, God, because all of this is truly Ephesians 3:20.

For each person who works to continue to find and use your voice, thank you for inspiring voice. Thank you for building—and fighting to build—lives worth living.

# Notes

## INTRODUCTION

1. Note: The examples used throughout the book are composites of clients I've worked with over the years, with details and names changed.
2. David J. Wasserstein, "A West-East Puzzle: On the History of the Proverb 'Speech in Silver, Silence in Golden,'" in *Compilation and Creation in Adab and Luġa: Studies in Memory of Naphtali Kinberg (1948–1997)*, ed. Albert Arazi, Joseph Sadan, and David J. Wasserstein (Tel Aviv: Eisenbrauns, 1999).
3. Jenni Radun et al., "Speech Is Special: The Stress Effects of Speech, Noise, and Silence During Tasks Requiring Concentration," *Indoor Air* 31, no. 1 (January 2021): 264–74, https://doi.org/10.1111/ina.12733.
4. L. Bernardi, C. Porta, and P. Sleight, "Cardiovascular, Cerebrovascular, and Respiratory Changes Induced by Different Types of Music in Musicians and Non-Musicians: The Importance of Silence," *Heart* 92, no. 4 (April 2006): 445–52, https://doi.org/10.1136/hrt.2005.064600.
5. Imke Kirste et. al., "Is Silence Golden? Effects of Auditory Stimuli and Their Absence on Adult Hippocampal Neurogenesis," *Brain Structure and Function* 220, no. 2 (March 2015): 1221–28, https://doi.org/10.1007/s00429-013-0679-3.
6. "The Big Sort," *Economist*, June 19, 2008, https://www.economist.com/united-states/2008/06/19/the-big-sort.

## CHAPTER 1: THE SILENCE WE LEARNED

1. Charles A. Nelson, Nathan A. Fox, and Charles H. Zeanah, *Romania's Abandoned Children: Deprivation, Brain Development, and the Struggle for Recovery* (Cambridge, MA: Harvard University Press, 2014).
2. "People: The Younger Generation," *Time*, November 5, 1951, http://content.time.com/time/subscriber/article/0,33009,856950,00.html.
3. Hannah Jane Parkinson, "From the Silent Generation to 'Snowflakes': Why You Need Friends of All Ages," *Guardian*, October 18, 2019, https://www.theguardian.com/lifeandstyle/2019/oct/18/silent-generation-to-snowflakes-why-you-need-friends-all-ages.
4. *Britannica Online*, s.v. "McCarthyism," by P. J. Achter, last updated December 5, 2022, https://www.britannica.com/topic/McCarthyism.

5. Mark Batterson and Richard Foth, *A Trip Around the Sun: Turning Your Everyday Life into the Adventure of a Lifetime* (Grand Rapids, MI: Baker Books, 2015).
6. AnnMarie D. Baines, *(Un)learning Disability: Recognizing and Changing Restrictive Views of Student Ability* (New York: Teachers College Press, 2014).
7. AnnMarie Baines, Diana Medina, and Caitlin Healy, *Amplify Student Voices: Equitable Practices to Build Confidence in the Classroom* (Arlington, VA: ASCD, 2023), chapter 3.
8. Ambreen Ahmed and Nawaz Ahmad, "Comparative Analysis of Rote Learning on High and Low Achievers in Graduate and Undergraduate Programs," *Journal of Education and Educational Development* 4 (2017): 111–29, https://www.researchgate.net/publication/317339196_Comparative_Analysis_of_Rote_Learning_on_High_and_Low_Achievers_in_Graduate_and_Undergraduate_Programs.
9. Kurt F. Geisinger, "21st Century Skills: What Are They and How Do We Assess Them?," *Applied Measurement in Education* 29, no. 4 (2016): 245–49, https://doi.org/10.1080/08957347.2016.1209207.
10. Amanda LaTasha Armstrong, "The Representation of Social Groups in U.S. Education Materials and Why It Matters," New America, February 16, 2022, http://newamerica.org/education-policy/briefs/the-representation-of-social-groups-in-us-education-materials-and-why-it-matters/.
11. Elizabeth Wolfe Morrison and Frances J. Milliken, "Organizational Silence: A Barrier to Change and Development in a Pluralistic World," *Academy of Management Review* 25, no. 4 (October 2000): 706–25, http://dx.doi.org/10.2307/259200.
12. Kerm Henricksen and Elizabeth Dayton, "Organizational Silence and Hidden Threats to Patient Safety," Health Services Research 41, no. 4, pt. 2 (August 2006): 1539–54, https://doi.org/10.1111%2Fj.1475-6773.2006.00564.x.
13. "Myths about Sexual Assault Reports," Brown University, BWell Health Promotion (2022), https://www.brown.edu/campus-life/health/services/promotion/sexual-assault-dating-violence/myths-about-sexual-assault-reports#:~:text=The%20study%20found%20that%204.5,however%2C%20it%20is%20very%20rare.
14. Free Dictionary, s.v. "Snitches get stitches," accessed March 23, 2022, https://idioms.thefreedictionary.com/snitches+get+stitches.
15. Ayah Young, "Deadly Silence: Stop Snitching's Fatal Legacy," *Wiretap*, March 28, 2008, https://web.archive.org/web/20080401135307/http:/www.wiretapmag.org/race/43473/.
16. USC Annenberg, "Inequality in 1,300 Popular Films: Examining Portrayals of Gender, Race/Ethnicity, LGBTQ & Disability from 2007 to 2019," Annenberg Inclusion Initiative (September 2020), https://assets.uscannenberg.org/docs/aii-inequality_1300_popular_films_09-08-2020.pdf.

## CHAPTER 2: THE PROBLEM WITH SILENCE

1. Associated Press, "Enron Whistleblower Tells of 'Crooked Company,'" NBC News, March 15, 2006, https://www.nbcnews.com/id/wbna11839694.
2. Dick Carozza, "Interview with Sherron Watkins: Constant Warning," *Fraud Magazine*, January/February 2007, https://www.fraud-magazine.com/article.aspx?id=583.
3. Albert O. Hirschman, *Exit, Voice, and Loyalty: Responses to Decline in Firms, Organizations, and States* (Cambridge, MA: Harvard University Press, 1970).
4. Gregory Moorhead and John R. Montanari, "An Empirical Investigation of the Groupthink Phenomenon," *Human Relations* 39, no. 5 (May 1986): 399–410, https://doi.org/10.1177/001872678603900502.

5. Silvia da Costa et al., "Obedience to Authority, Cognitive and Affective Responses and Leadership Style in Relation to a Non-Normative Order: The Milgram Experiment" ("*Obediencia a la Autoridad, Respuestas Cognitivas y Afectivas y Estilo de Liderazgo en Relación a una Orden no Normativa: El Experimento de Milgram*"), *Revista de Psicología* 39, no. 2 (2021): 717–44, https://doi.org/10.18800/psico.202102.008.

6. Deepa Purushothaman and Valerie Rein, "Workplace Toxicity Is Not Just a Mental Health Issue," *MIT Sloan Management Review*, January 18, 2023, https://sloanreview.mit.edu/article/workplace-toxicity-is-not-just-a-mental-health-issue/.

7. Maria Ritter, "Silence as the Voice of Trauma," *American Journal of Psychoanalysis* 74 (2014): 176–94, https://doi.org/10.1057/ajp.2014.5.

8. E. D. Lister, "Forced Silence: A Neglected Dimension of Trauma," *American Journal of Psychiatry* 139, no. 7 (July 1982): 872–76, https://doi.org/10.1176/ajp.139.7.872.

9. Bessel van der Kolk, *The Body Keeps the Score: Brain, Mind, and Body in the Healing of Trauma* (New York: Penguin Books, September 2015).

10. Valerie Purdie-Vaughns and Richard P. Eibach, "Intersectional Invisibility: The Distinctive Advantages and Disadvantages of Multiple Subordinate-Group Identities," *Sex Roles* 59 (2008): 377–91, https://doi.org/10.1007/s11199-008-9424-4.

11. Xochitl Gonzalez, "Why Do Rich People Love Quiet?," *Atlantic*, August 1, 2022, https://www.theatlantic.com/magazine/archive/2022/09/let-brooklyn-be-loud/670600/.

12. Elizabeth K. Laney, M. Elizabeth Lewis Hall, Tamara L. Anderson, and Michele M. Willingham, "Becoming a Mother: The Influence of Motherhood on Women's Identity Development," *Identity* 15, no. 2 (2015): 126–45, https://doi.org/10.1080/15283488.2015.1023440.

13. Hazel M. MacRae, "Women and Caring: Constructing Self Through Others," *Journal of Women & Aging* 7, nos. 1–2 (1995): 145–67, https://doi.org/10.1300/J074v07n01_11.

14. Karen Rinaldi, "Motherhood Isn't Sacrifice, It's Selfishness," Opinion, *New York Times*, August 4, 2017, https://www.nytimes.com/2017/08/04/opinion/sunday/motherhood-family-sexism-sacrifice.html.

15. Anne Helen Petersen, "'Other Countries Have Social Safety Nets. The U.S. Has Women,'" Culture Study, November 11, 2020, https://annehelen.substack.com/p/other-countries-have-social-safety.

16. Craig Timberg, "New Whistleblower Claims Facebook Allowed Hate, Illegal Activity to Go Unchecked," *Washington Post*, October 22, 2021, https://www.washingtonpost.com/technology/2021/10/22/facebook-new-whistleblower-complaint/.

17. Julie Miller, "Paying the Price for Blowing the Whistle," *New York Times*, February 12, 1995, https://www.nytimes.com/1995/02/12/nyregion/paying-the-price-for-blowing-the-whistle.html.

18. "Double Pain," Super Mario Wiki, last edited May 10, 2022, https://www.mariowiki.com/Double_Pain.

19. Julianne Holt-Lunstad et al., "Loneliness and Social Isolation as Risk Factors for Mortality: A Meta-Analytic Review," *Perspectives on Psychological Science* 10, no. 2 (March 2015): 227–37, https://doi.org/10.1177/1745691614568352.

20. Stephanie Cacioppo et al., "Loneliness: Clinical Import and Interventions," *Perspectives on Psychological Science* 10, no. 2 (March 2015): 238–49, https://doi.org/10.1177/1745691615570616.

21. Emma Bassett and Spencer Moore, "Mental Health and Social Capital: Social Capital as a Promising Initiative to Improving the Mental Health of Communi-

ties," in *Current Topics in Public Health,* ed. Alfonso J. Rodriguez-Morales (London: IntechOpen, May 2013), http://dx.doi.org/10.5772/53501.

22. James W. Pennebaker, *Opening Up: The Healing Power of Expressing Emotions* (New York: Guilford Press, 1997).

23. David A. Goldstein and Michael H. Antoni, "The Distribution of Repressive Coping Styles Among Non-Metastatic and Metastatic Breast Cancer Patients as Compared to Non-Cancer Patients," *Psychology and Health* 3, no. 4 (1989): 245–58, https://doi.org/10.1080/08870448908400384.

24. Jainish Patel and Pritish Patel, "Consequences of Repression of Emotion: Physical Health, Mental Health and General Well Being," *International Journal of Psychotherapy Practice and Research* 1, no. 3 (February 2019): 16–21, http://dx.doi.org/10.14302/issn.2574-612X.ijpr-18-2564.

25. J. J. Gross and O. P. John, "Individual Differences in Two Emotion Regulation Processes: Implications for Affect, Relationships, and Well-Being," *Journal of Personality and Social Psychology* 85, no. 2 (August 2003): 348–62, https://doi.org/10.1037/0022-3514.85.2.348.

26. David Matsumoto et al., "The Contribution of Individualism Vs. Collectivism to Cross-National Differences in Display Rules," *Asian Journal of Social Psychology* 1, no. 2 (1998): 147–65, https://psycnet.apa.org/doi/10.1111/1467-839X.00010.

27. Heejung S. Kim et al., "Gene-Culture Interaction: Oxytocin Receptor Polymorphism (OXTR) and Emotion Regulation," *Social Psychological and Personality Science* 2, no. 6 (November 2011): 665–72, https://doi.org/10.1177/1948550611405854.

28. P. Cramer, "Defense Mechanisms in Psychology Today: Further Processes for Adaptation," *American Psychologist* 55, no. 6 (June 2000): 637–46, https://psycnet.apa.org/doi/10.1037/0003-066X.55.6.637.

29. Matteo Cinelli et al., "The Echo Chamber Effect on Social Media," *PNAS* 118, no. 9 (March 2021), https://doi.org/10.1073/pnas.2023301118.

30. "Getting Muslim Representation Right," Pillars Fund, August 2021, https://pillarsfund.org/content/uploads/2021/08/Getting-Muslim-Representation-Right.pdf.

31. Boaz Munro, "Dear American Progressives: Your Jewish Friends Are Terrified by Your Silence," *An Injustice!,* May 31, 2021, https://aninjusticemag.com/dear-american-progressives-your-jewish-friends-are-terrified-b24068fcf488.

32. Tiffany Bluhm, *Prey Tell: Why We Silence Women Who Tell the Truth and How Everyone Can Speak Up* (Ada, MI: Brazos Press, 2021).

## CHAPTER 3: WHEN SILENCE MAKES SENSE

1. Ryan Pendell, "5 Ways Managers Can Stop Employee Turnover," Gallup, November 10, 2021, https://www.gallup.com/workplace/357104/ways-managers-stop-employee-turnover.aspx.

2. Quantum Workplace and Fierce Conversations, "The State of Miscommunication: 6 Insights on Effective Workplace Communication," Greater Pensacola Society for Human Resource Management, June 2021, http://www.gpshrm.org/resources/Documents/The-State-of-Miscommunication.pdf.

3. Pooja Lakshmin, *Real Self-Care: A Transformative Program for Redefining Wellness* (New York: Penguin Life, March 2023).

4. Dan W. Grupe and Jack B. Nitschke, "Uncertainty and Anticipation in Anxiety: An Integrated Neurobiological and Psychological Perspective," *Nature Reviews Neuroscience* 14 (2013): 488–501, https://doi.org/10.1038/nrn3524.

5. R. Nicholas Carleton, "Fear of the Unknown: One Fear to Rule Them All?," *Journal of Anxiety Disorders* 41 (June 2016): 5–21, https://doi.org/10.1016/j.janxdis.2016 .03.011.

6. Aysa Gray, "The Bias of 'Professionalism' Standards," *Stanford Social Innovation Review* (2019), https://doi.org/10.48558/TDWC-4756.

7. Adam Galinsky, "How to Speak Up for Yourself," Ideas.TED, February 17, 2017, https://ideas.ted.com/how-to-speak-up-for-yourself/.

8. Emma Hinchliffe, "The Female CEOs on This Year's Fortune 500 Just Broke Three All-Time Records," *Fortune*, June 2, 2021, https://fortune.com/2021/06 /02/female-ceos-fortune-500-2021-women-ceo-list-roz-brewer-walgreens-karen -lynch-cvs-thasunda-brown-duckett-tiaa/.

9. Allison Moser, "How to Improve Gender Diversity in the Workplace," Culture Amp, accessed May 11, 2022, https://www.cultureamp.com/blog/improving-the-gender -diversity-of-work-teams.

10. Sundiatu Dixon-Fyle, Kevin Dolan, Dame Vivian Hunt, and Sara Prince, "Diversity Wins: Why Inclusion Matters," McKinsey & Company, May 19, 2020, https:// www.mckinsey.com/featured-insights/diversity-and-inclusion/diversity-wins-how -inclusion-matters.

11. Sarah Beaulieu, *Breaking the Silence Habit: A Practical Guide to Uncomfortable Conversations in the #MeToo Workplace* (Oakland, CA: Berrett-Koehler Publishers, 2020), 125.

12. Courtney L. McCluney et al., "The Costs of Code-Switching," *Harvard Business Review*, November 15, 2019, https://hbr.org/2019/11/the-costs-of-codeswitching.

13. Gregory M. Walton, Mary C. Murphy, and Ann Marie Ryan, "Stereotype Threat in Organizations: Implications for Equity and Performance," *Annual Review of Organizational Psychology and Organizational Behavior* 2 (April 2015): 523–50, https://doi.org/10.1146/annurev-orgpsych-032414-111322.

14. P. F. Hewlin, "Wearing the Cloak: Antecedents and Consequences of Creating Facades of Conformity," *Journal of Applied Psychology* 94, no. 3 (May 2009): 727–41, https://doi.org/10.1037/a0015228.

15. Miller McPherson, Lynn Smith-Lovin, and James M. Cook, "Birds of a Feather: Homophily in Social Networks," *Annual Review of Sociology* 27 (August 2001): 415–44, https://doi.org/10.1146/annurev.soc.27.1.415.

16. Cameron Anderson and Gavin J. Kilduff, "The Pursuit of Status in Social Groups," *Current Directions in Psychological Science* 18, no. 5 (October 2009): 295–98, https://doi.org/10.1111/j.1467-8721.2009.01655.x.

17. Amy Edmondson, "Psychological Safety and Learning Behavior in Work Teams," *Administrative Science Quarterly* 44, no. 2 (June 1999): 350–83, https://doi.org /10.2307/2666999.

18. Sharmila Sivalingam, "The Brain: Saboteur or Success Partner? Exploring the Role of Neuroscience in the Workplace," *Journal of Humanities and Social Sciences Research* 2, no. 1 (July 2020): 5–10, http://dx.doi.org/10.37534/bp.jhssr .2020.v2.n1.id1019.p5.

19. Bessel van der Kolk, *The Body Keeps the Score: Brain, Mind, and Body in the Healing of Trauma* (New York: Penguin Books, September 2015).

20. Naomi I. Eisenberger, "The Neural Bases of Social Pain: Evidence for Shared Representations with Physical Pain," *Psychosomatic Medicine* 74, no. 2 (February 2012): 126–35, https://doi.org/10.1097%2FPSY.0b013e3182464dd1.

21. APA Dictionary of Psychology, s.v. "Self-preservation instinct," https://dictionary .apa.org/self-preservation-instinct.

22. van der Kolk, *The Body Keeps the Score.*

23. Aimaloghi Eromosele, "There Is No Self-Care Without Community Care," URGE,

November 10, 2020, https://urge.org/there-is-no-self-care-without-community-care/.

24. Patricia Worthy, "Black Women Say Goodbye to the Job and Hello to Their Own Businesses," *Guardian*, February 12, 2022, https://www.theguardian.com/business/2022/feb/12/black-women-say-goodbye-to-the-job-and-hello-to-their-own-businesses.

25. Amy Wilkins, "Not Out to Start a Revolution: Race, Gender, and Emotional Restraint Among Black University Men," *Journal of Contemporary Ethnography* 41, no. 1 (2012): 34–65, https://journals.sagepub.com/doi/abs/10.1177/0891241611433053.

26. Anukit Chakraborty, "Present Bias," *Econometrica: Journal of the Econometric Society* 89, no. 4 (July 2021): 1921–61, https://doi.org/10.3982/ECTA16467.

27. Amy C. Edmondson, *The Fearless Organization: Creating Psychological Safety in the Workplace for Learning, Innovation, and Growth* (Hoboken, NJ: John Wiley & Sons, 2018).

28. James W. Moore, "What Is the Sense of Agency and Why Does it Matter?," *Frontiers in Psychology* 7 (August 2016): 1272, https://doi.org/10.3389/fpsyg.2016.01272.

29. Albert Bandura, "Toward a Psychology of Human Agency," *Perspectives on Psychological Science* 1, no. 2 (June 2006): 164–80, https://doi.org/10.1111/j.1745-6916.2006.00011.x.

## CHAPTER 4: HOW WE SILENCE OURSELVES

1. James L. Gibson and Joseph L. Sutherland, "Keeping Your Mouth Shut: Spiraling Self-Censorship in the United States," *Political Studies Quarterly 2023* (forthcoming; posted June 1, 2020), https://dx.doi.org/10.2139/ssrn.3647099.

2. Megan Call, "Why Is Behavior Change So Hard?," Accelerate, January 31, 2022, http://accelerate.uofuhealth.utah.edu/resilience/why-is-behavior-change-so-hard.

3. Maria Masters, "70 Dieting Statistics You Should Know," Livestrong, June 8, 2021, https://www.livestrong.com/article/13764583-diet-statistics/.

4. Chris Argyris, "Double Loop Learning in Organizations," *Harvard Business Review*, September 1977, https://hbr.org/1977/09/double-loop-learning-in-organizations.

5. Rick van Baaren et al., "Where Is the Love? The Social Aspects of Mimicry," *Philosophical Transactions of the Royal Society of London B* 364, no. 1528 (August 2009): 2381–89, https://doi.org/10.1098/rstb.2009.0057.

6. Nicolas Guéguen, Céline Jacob, and Angelique Martin, "Mimicry in Social Interaction: Its Effect on Human Judgment and Behavior," *European Journal of Social Sciences* 8, no. 2 (April 2009), https://www.researchgate.net/publication/228514642.

7. David J. Lieberman, *Get Anyone to Do Anything and Never Feel Powerless Again: Psychological Secrets to Predict, Control, and Influence Every Situation* (New York: St. Martin's Press, 2010).

8. Pilita Clark, "It's OK to Be Quiet in Meetings," *Financial Times*, April 30, 2022, https://www.ft.com/content/6d5942a2-a13a-49ea-a833-a6d5ce780ae3.

9. Neil G. MacLaren et. al, "Testing the Babble Hypothesis: Speaking Time Predicts Leader Emergence in Small Groups," *Leadership Quarterly* 31, no. 5 (October 2020), https://doi.org/10.1016/j.leaqua.2020.101409.

10. Andrew F. Hayes, Carroll J. Glynn, and James Shanahan, "Willingness to Self-Censor: A Construct and Measurement Tool for Public Opinion Research," *International Journal of Public Opinion Research* 17, no. 3 (Autumn 2005): 298–323, https://doi.org/10.1093/ijpor/edh073.

11. Kerri Smith, "Brain Makes Decisions Before You Even Know It," *Nature*, April 11, 2008, www.nature.com, https://doi.org/10.1038/news.2008.751.

12. Malcolm Gladwell, *Outliers: The Story of Success* (New York: Little, Brown and Company, 2008).

13. Sik Hung Ng and James J. Bradac, *Power in Language: Verbal Communication and Social Influence* (London: Sage Publications, 1993).

14. B. Robey, "Sons and Daughters in China," *Asian and Pacific Census Forum* 12, no. 2 (November 1985): 1–5, https://pubmed.ncbi.nlm.nih.gov/12267834/.

15. Ute Fischer and Judith Orasanu, "Cultural Diversity and Crew Communication," paper presented at the Fiftieth Astronautical Congress, Amsterdam, The Netherlands, October 1999.

16. Brené Brown, *Dare to Lead: Brave Work. Tough Conversations. Whole Hearts.* (New York: Random House, 2018).

17. Lisa K. Fazio, David G. Rand, and Gordon Pennycook, "Repetition Increases Perceived Truth Equally for Plausible and Implausible Statements," *Psychonomic Bulletin & Review* 26, no. 5 (October 2019): 1705–10, https://doi.org/10.3758/s13423-019-01651-4.

18. Giulio Perrotta, "The Reality Plan and the Subjective Construction of One's Perception: The Strategic Theoretical Model Among Sensations, Perceptions, Defence Mechanisms, Needs, Personal Constructs, Beliefs System, Social Influences and Systematic Errors," *Journal of Clinical Research and Reports* 1, no. 1 (December 2019), http://dx.doi.org/10.31579/JCRR/2019/001.

## CHAPTER 5: HOW WE SILENCE OTHERS

1. Michael C. Anderson and Simon Hanslmayr, "Neural Mechanisms of Motivated Forgetting," *Trends in Cognitive Sciences* 18, no. 6 (June 2014): 279–92, https://doi.org/10.1016/j.tics.2014.03.002.

2. Ryan W. Carlson et al., "Motivated Misremembering of Selfish Decisions," *Nature Communications* 11, no. 2100 (April 2020), https://doi.org/10.1038/s41467-020-15602-4.

3. Megan Reitz and John Higgins, "Managers, You're More Intimidating Than You Think," *Harvard Business Review*, July 18, 2019, https://hbr.org/2019/07/managers-youre-more-intimidating-than-you-think.

4. Sarah Kocher, "Most Employees Are Too Intimidated to Talk to Their Boss About Work Issues," *New York Post*, March 2, 2020, https://nypost.com/2020/03/02/most-employees-are-too-intimidated-to-talk-to-their-boss-about-work-issues/.

5. RACI is a different project management tool in which parties to a project are assigned one of four roles: Responsible (R), Accountable (A), Consulted (C), and Informed (I). There are a multitude of derivatives including RAPID, PARIS, and other acronyms. All get at a similar idea of clarifying roles and expectations.

6. Felipe Csaszar and Alfredo Enrione, "When Consensus Hurts the Company," *MIT Sloan Management Review* 56, no. 3 (Spring 2015): 17–20, https://sloanreview.mit.edu/article/when-consensus-hurts-the-company/.

7. Naomi Havron et al., "The Effect of Older Siblings on Language Development as a Function of Age Difference and Sex," *Psychological Science* 30, no. 9 (August 2019): 1333–43, https://doi.org/10.1177/0956797619861436.

8. "Americans Check Their Phones 96 Times a Day," Asurion, November 21, 2019, https://www.asurion.com/press-releases/americans-check-their-phones-96-times-a-day; "The New Normal: Phone Use Is Up Nearly 4-Fold Since 2019, According to Tech Care Company Asurion," Asurion, https://www.asurion.com/connect/news/tech-usage/; Burt Rea, "Simplification of Work: The Coming Revolution," Deloitte Insights, February 27, 2015, https://www2.deloitte.com/us/en/insights

/focus/human-capital-trends/2015/work-simplification-human-capital-trends
-2015.html.

9. Matthew D. Lieberman, "Reflexive and Reflective Judgment Processes: A Social
Cognitive Neuroscience Approach," in *Social Judgments: Implicit and Explicit
Processes*, ed. Joseph P. Forgas, Kipling D. Williams, and William von Hippel
(Cambridge: Cambridge University Press, 2011), 44–67.

10. Bob Nease, *The Power of Fifty Bits: The New Science of Turning Good Intentions
into Positive Results* (New York: Harper Business, 2016).

11. Nease, *The Power of Fifty Bits*.

12. Daniz Vatansever, David K. Menon, and Emmanuel A. Stamatakis, "Default Mode
Contributions to Automated Information Processing," *Biological Sciences* 114, no.
48 (October 2017): 12821–26, https://doi.org/10.1073/pnas.1710521114.

13. Malcolm Gladwell, *Blink: The Power of Thinking Without Thinking* (New York:
Little, Brown and Company, 2005).

14. Shouhang Yin et al., "Automatic Prioritization of Self-Referential Stimuli in Working Memory," *Psychological Science* 30, no. 3 (March 2019): 415–23, https://doi
.org/10.1177/0956797618818483.

15. Carey Nieuwhof, *At Your Best: How to Get Time, Energy, and Priorities Working in
Your Favor* (New York: WaterBrook/Penguin, 2021).

16. Kelly Dickerson, Peter Gerhardstein, and Alecia Moser, "The Role of the Human
Mirror Neuron System in Supporting Communication in a Digital World," *Frontiers
in Psychology* 12, no. 8 (May 2017): 698, https://doi.org/10.3389/fpsyg.2017.00698.

17. Douglas Stone and Sheila Heen, *Thanks for the Feedback: The Science and Art of
Receiving Feedback Well* (New York: Viking, 2014).

## CHAPTER 6: FIND YOUR VOICE

1. Gary Burtless, "The Case for Randomized Field Trials in Economic and Policy
Research," *Journal of Economic Perspectives* 9, no. 2 (Spring 1995): 63–84, http://
dx.doi.org/10.1257/jep.9.2.63.

2. Ayelet Gneezy, Alex Imas, and Ania Jaroszewicz, "The Impact of Agency on Time
and Risk Preferences," *Nature Communications* 11, no. 1 (May 2020): 2665,
https://doi.org/10.1038/s41467-020-16440-0.

3. Amanda Bower and James G. Maxham, "Return Shipping Policies of Online Re-
tailers: Normative Assumptions and the Long-Term Consequences of Fee and
Free Returns," *Journal of Marketing* 76, no. 5 (September 2012): 110–24, https://
doi.org/10.1509/jm.10.0419.

4. Stacy L. Wood, "Remote Purchase Environments: The Influence of Return Policy
Leniency on Two-Stage Decision Processes," *Journal of Marketing Research* 38,
no. 2 (May 2001): 157–69, https://doi.org/10.1509/jmkr.38.2.157.18847.

5. K. Savitsky, N. Epley, and T. Gilovich, "Do Others Judge Us as Harshly as We
Think? Overestimating the Impact of Our Failures, Shortcomings, and Mishaps,"
*Journal of Personality and Social Psychology* 81, no. 1 (1970): 44–56, https://doi
.org/10.1037/0022-3514.81.1.44.

6. Susan Nolen-Hoeksema, *Women Who Think Too Much: How to Break Free of
Overthinking and Reclaim Your Life* (New York: Henry Holt, 2003).

7. Susan Nolen-Hoeksema, Blair E. Wisco, and Sonja Lyubomirsky, "Rethinking
Rumination," *Perspectives on Psychological Science* 3, no. 5 (September 2008):
400–424, https://doi.org/10.1111/j.1745-6924.2008.00088.x.

8. Matthew D. Lieberman et al., "Putting Feelings into Words: Affect Labeling Dis-
rupts Amygdala Activity in Response to Affective Stimuli," *Psychological Science*
18, no. 5 (May 2007): 421–28, https://doi.org/10.1111/j.1467-9280.2007.01916.x.

9. Vocabulary.com, s.v. "Sounding board," accessed September 2, 2022, https://www.vocabulary.com/dictionary/sounding%20board.

10. Justin P. Boren, "The Relationships Between Co-Rumination, Social Support, Stress, and Burnout Among Working Adults," *Management Communication Quarterly*, 28, no. 1 (February 2014): 3s–25, https://doi.org/10.1177/0893318913509283.

## CHAPTER 7: USE YOUR VOICE

1. Nancy Baym, Jonathan Larson, and Ronnie Martin, "What a Year of WFH Has Done to Our Relationships at Work," *Harvard Business Review*, March 22, 2021, https://hbr.org/2021/03/what-a-year-of-wfh-has-done-to-our-relationships-at-work.

2. Batia Ben Hador, "How Intra-Organizational Social Capital Influences Employee Performance," *Journal of Management Development* 35, no. 9 (October 2016): 1119–33, https://doi.org/10.1108/JMD-12-2015-0172.

3. Alisa Cohn, "How Cofounders Can Prevent Their Relationship from Derailing," *Harvard Business Review*, April 11, 2022, https://hbr.org/2022/04/how-cofounders -can-prevent-their-relationship-from-derailing.

4. Esteban Ortiz-Ospina and Max Roser, "Marriages and Divorces," Our World in Data, accessed April 20, 2023, https://ourworldindata.org/marriages-and-divorces.

5. Zulekha Nathoo, "The People Penalised for Expressing Feelings at Work," Equality Matters, BBC, November 1, 2021, https://www.bbc.com/worklife/article /20211029-the-people-penalised-for-expressing-feelings-at-work.

6. Stephanie M. Ortiz and Chad R. Mandala, "'There Is Queer Inequity, But I Pick to Be Happy': Racialized Feeling Rules and Diversity Regimes in University LGBTQ Resource Centers," *Du Bois Review: Social Science Research on Race* 18, no. 2 (April 2021): 347–64, https://doi.org/10.1017/S1742058X21000096.

7. Adia Harvey Wingfield, "Are Some Emotions Marked 'Whites Only'? Racialized Feeling Rules in Professional Workplaces," *Social Problems* 57, no. 2 (May 2010): 251–68, https://doi.org/10.1525/sp.2010.57.2.251.

8. Moshe Zeidner, Gerald Matthews, and Richard D. Roberts, "Emotional Intelligence in the Workplace: A Critical Review," *Applied Psychology* 53, no. 3 (June 2004): 371–99, https://doi.org/10.1111/j.1464-0597.2004.00176.x.

9. Michael R. Parke and Myeong-Gu Seo, "The Role of Affect Climate in Organizational Effectiveness," *Academy of Management Review* 42, no. 2 (January 2016): 334–60, https://psycnet.apa.org/doi/10.5465/amr.2014.0424.

10. Sigal Barsade and Olivia A. O'Neill, "Manage Your Emotional Culture," *Harvard Business Review*, January–February 2016, https://hbr.org/2016/01/manage-your -emotional-culture.

11. Elizabeth Bernstein, "Speaking Up Is Hard to Do: Researchers Explain Why," *Wall Street Journal*, February 7, 2012, https://www.wsj.com/articles/SB1000142 4052970204136404577207020525853492.

12. Kelly Dickerson, Peter Gerhardstein, and Alecia Moser, "The Role of the Human Mirror Neuron System in Supporting Communication in a Digital World," *Frontiers in Psychology* 12, no. 8 (May 2017): 698, https://doi.org/10.3389/fpsyg.2017.00698.

13. R. Hollander-Blumoff and T. R. Tyler, "Procedural Justice in Negotiation: Procedural Fairness, Outcome Acceptance, and Integrative Potential," *Law & Social Inquiry* 33, no. 2 (Spring 2008): 473–500, https://doi.org/10.1111/j.1747-4469.2008.00110.x.

## CHAPTER 8: HOW TO SPEAK UP

1. Andrea Downey, "Germ Alert: This Is How Many Germs Are Lurking in Your Bathroom, and You'll Be Horrified at the Dirtiest Spot," *The Sun*, April 7, 2017,

https://www.thesun.co.uk/living/3272186/this-is-how-many-germs-are
-lurking-in-your-bathroom-and-youll-be-horrified-at-the-dirtiest-spot/.

2. Adrian Hearn, "Flushed Away: Images Show Bacteria Propelled from Toilets
When Flushing with Lid Open," *Independent*, November 2, 2020, https://www
.independent.co.uk/news/uk/home-news/bacteria-toilets-flush-lid-closed
-b1535481.html.

3. Simon Sinek, *Start with Why: How Great Leaders Inspire Everyone to Take Action*
(New York: Portfolio/Penguin, 2009).

4. Robert Kegan and Lisa Laskow Lahey, *Immunity to Change: How to Overcome It
and Unlock the Potential in Yourself and Your Organization* (Boston: Harvard
Business Review Press, 2009).

5. Patricia Satterstrom, Michaela Kerrissey, and Julia DiBenigno, "The Voice Cultivation Process: How Team Members Can Help Upward Voice Live On to Imple-
mentation," *Administrative Science Quarterly* 66, no. 2 (June 2021): 380–425,
https://doi.org/10.1177/0001839220962795.

6. Satterstrom, Kerrissey, and DiBenigno, "The Voice Cultivation Process."

## CHAPTER 9: STOP SILENCING PEOPLE

1. Clay Drinko, "We're Worse at Listening Than We Realize," *Psychology Today*, August 4, 2021, https://www.psychologytoday.com/us/blog/play-your-way-sane
/202108/were-worse-listening-we-realize.

2. Bob Sullivan and Hugh Thompson, "Now Hear This! Most People Stink at Listening [Excerpt]," *Scientific American*, May 3, 2013, https://www.scientificamerican
.com/article/plateau-effect-digital-gadget-distraction-attention/.

3. Nathanael J. Fast, Ethan R. Burris, and Caroline A. Bartel, "Managing to Stay in
the Dark: Managerial Self-Efficacy, Ego Defensiveness, and the Aversion to Employee Voice," *Academy of Management Journal* 57, no. 4 (2014): 1013–34, https://
doi.org/10.5465/amj.2012.0393.

4. Elizabeth Wolfe Morrison and Frances J. Milliken, "Organizational Silence: A
Barrier to Change and Development in a Pluralistic World," *Academy of Management Review* 25, no. 4 (October 2000): 706–25, http://dx.doi.org/10.2307/259200.

5. Emile G. Bruneau and Rebecca Saxe, "The Power of Being Heard: The Benefits of
'Perspective-Giving' in the Context of Intergroup Conflict," *Journal of Experi-
mental Social Psychology* 48, no. 4 (July 2012): 855–66, https://doi.org/10.1016
/j.jesp.2012.02.017.

6. Patricia Satterstrom, Michaela Kerrissey, and Julia DiBenigno, "The Voice Cultivation Process: How Team Members Can Help Upward Voice Live On to Implemen-
tation," *Administrative Science Quarterly* 66, no. 2 (June 2021): 380–425, https://
doi.org/10.1177/0001839220962795.

## CHAPTER 10: CHANGE THE SYSTEM

1. Ross D. Arnold and Jon P. Wade, "A Definition of Systems Thinking: A Systems
Approach," *Procedia Computer Science* 44 (2015): 669–78, https://doi.org/10.1016
/j.procs.2015.03.050.

2. Karen L. Fingerman and Eric Bermann, "Applications of Family Systems Theory
to the Study of Adulthood," *International Journal of Aging and Human Development* 51, no. 1 (July 2000): 5–29, https://doi.org/10.2190/7TF8-WB3F-TMWG
-TT3K.

3. Orly Lobel, "NDAs Are Out of Control. Here's What Needs to Change," *Harvard*

*Business Review*, January 30, 2018, https://hbr.org/2018/01/ndas-are-out-of
-control-heres-what-needs-to-change.

4. Andreas Leibbrandt and John A. List, "Do Women Avoid Salary Negotiations?
Evidence from a Large-Scale Natural Field Experiment," *Management Science*
61, no. 9 (September 2015): 2016–24, https://doi.org/10.1287/mnsc.2014.1994.

5. D. A. Small, M. Gelfand, L. Babcock, and H. Gettman, "Who Goes to the Bargain-
ing Table? The Influence of Gender and Framing on the Initiation of Negotiation,"
*Journal of Personality and Social Psychology* 93, no. 4 (2007): 600–613, https://
doi.org/10.1037/0022-3514.93.4.600.

6. Hannah Riley Bowles, Linda Babcock, and Lei Lai, "Social Incentives for Gender
Differences in the Propensity to Initiate Negotiations: Sometimes It Does Hurt to
Ask," *Organizational Behavior and Human Decision Processes* 103, no. 1 (May
2007): 84–103, https://doi.org/10.1016/j.obhdp.2006.09.001.

7. Laura Kray, Jessica Kennedy, and Margaret Lee, "Now, Women Do Ask: A Call to
Update Beliefs about the Gender Pay Gap," Academy of Management Discoveries
(August 2023), https://doi.org/10.5465/amd.2022.0021.

8. Linda Babcock and Sara Laschever, *Women Don't Ask: Gender and the Negotiation
Divide* (Princeton, NJ: Princeton University Press, 2003).

9. #NotMe (website), NotMe Solutions, Inc., https://not-me.com/.

10. Mary Kovach, "Leader Influence: A Research Review of French & Raven's (1959)
Power Dynamics," *Journal of Values-Based Leadership* 13, no. 2 (2020): article 15,
https://doi.org/10.22543/0733.132.1312.

11. Heath Hardage Lee, "Wives of Vietnam POWs Were Told to Keep Quiet About
Their Husbands' Captivity. Here's What Convinced Them to Go Public," *Time*,
April 2, 2019, https://time.com/5562257/vietnam-pow-wives-go-public/.

12. Jason Breslow, "The Families of Americans Who Are Wrongfully Detained Are
Very Much Done Being Quiet," NPR, August 4, 2022, https://www.npr.org/2022
/07/29/1114225672/brittney-griner-americans-wrongfully-detained-bring-our
-families-home-campaign.

13. Heath Hardage Lee, *The League of Wives: The Untold Story of the Women Who
Took On the U.S. Government to Bring Their Husbands Home* (New York: St. Martin's Press, 2019).

14. Bernice A. Pescosolido et al., "Trends in Public Stigma of Mental Illness in the
US, 1996–2018," *JAMA Network Open* 4, no. 12 (December 2021), https://doi.org
/10.1001/jamanetworkopen.2021.40202.

15. Pescosolido, "Trends in Public Stigma of Mental Illness in the US, 1996–2018."

16. "Stigma, Prejudice and Discrimination Against People with Mental Illness,"
American Psychiatric Association, accessed November 4, 2022, https://www
.psychiatry.org/patients-families/stigma-and-discrimination.

17. Laura Anthony, "Warriors President Reveals Meaning Behind 'Strength in Numbers' Slogan," ABC7 News, KGO-TV San Francisco, May 11, 2016, https://abc7news
.com/warriors-president-talks-about-meaning-behind-strength-in-numbers
-slogan-golden-state-rick-welts-reveals-success/1334388/.

18. Kyle Irving, "When Was the Last Time the Warriors Won the NBA Championship? Golden State Looking to Win Fourth Title in Eight Years," *Sporting News*,
June 16, 2022, https://www.sportingnews.com/us/nba/news/last-time-warriors
-won-nba-championship/wgbh4rieduxz3zwjrl2iplxx.

19. Doug Smith, "Golden State Warriors Thrive on Fans' Energy at Oracle Arena,"
*Toronto Star*, November 17, 2015, https://www.thestar.com/sports/raptors/2015
/11/17/golden-state-warriors-thrive-on-fans-energy-at-oracle-arena.html.

20. Louise C. Hawkley and John P. Capitanio, "Perceived Social Isolation, Evolutionary

Fitness and Health Outcomes: A Lifespan Approach," *Philosophical Transactions of the Royal Society B* 370, no. 1669 (May 2015), http://doi.org/10.1098/rstb.2014.0114.

21. Yoon-Sik Jung, Hyo-Sun Jung, and Hye-Hyun Yoon, "The Effects of Workplace Loneliness on the Psychological Detachment and Emotional Exhaustion of Hotel Employees," *International Journal of Environmental Research and Public Health* 19, no. 9 (April 2022): 5228, https://doi.org/10.3390/ijerph19095228.

22. Janine E. Janosky et al., "Coalitions for Impacting the Health of a Community: The Summit County, Ohio, Experience," *Population Health Management* 16, no. 4 (August 2013): 246–54, https://doi.org/10.1089/pop.2012.0083.

23. Janice D. Yoder, "Looking Beyond Numbers: The Effects of Gender Status, Job Prestige, and Occupational Gender-Typing on Tokenism Processes," *Social Psychology Quarterly* 57, no. 2 (June 1994): 150–59, https://doi.org/10.2307/2786708.

24. Nilofer Merchant, "How to Effect Change at Work When You're 'The First' or 'The Only,'" *Yes & Know* (blog), Nilofer Merchant, November 8, 2017, https://nilofermerchant.com/2017/11/08/how-to-effect-change-at-work-when-youre-the-first-or-the-only/.

25. Kastalia Medrano, "Obama's Female Staffers Make Shine Theory Shine," *Time*, September 14, 2006, https://time.com/4493715/obama-staff-shine-theory/.

26. Cole Horton, "The World's Youngest Billionaires 2022: 12 Under Age 30," *Forbes*, April 5, 2022, https://www.forbes.com/sites/colehorton/2022/04/05/the-worlds-youngest-billionaires-2022-12-under-age-30/?sh=211b5d07e63b.

27. Sean Silcoff, "Boris Wertz's Version One Raises Two Venture Funds After Blowout Year Fuelled by Big Crypto Gains," *Globe and Mail*, June 8, 2021, https://www.theglobeandmail.com/business/article-boris-wertzs-version-one-raises-two-venture-funds-after-blowout-year/.

28. Arlene Kaplan Daniels, "Invisible Work," *Social Problems* 34, no. 5 (December 1987): 403–15, https://doi.org/10.2307/800538.

29. Ivanhoe Newswire, "Women and Invisible Work: It's Time to Be Seen and Heard," KSAT, January 11, 2022, https://www.ksat.com/news/local/2022/01/11/women-and-invisible-work-its-time-to-be-seen-and-heard/.

30. "Redistribute Unpaid Work," UN Women, accessed October 21, 2022, https://www.unwomen.org/en/news/in-focus/csw61/redistribute-unpaid-work#notes.

31. Molly Callahan and Lia Petronio, "Researcher Uses Hacked Studio Data to Prove Racially Diverse Casts Are More Profitable," Phys.Org, December 7, 2018, https://phys.org/news/2018-12-hacked-studio-racially-diverse-profitable.html#jCp.

32. Lindsey Bahr and Associated Press, "'Black Panther: Wakanda Forever' Soars to Second Biggest Opening of 2022 with $180 Million in Ticket Sales," *Fortune*, November 13, 2022, https://fortune.com/2022/11/13/black-panther-wakanda-forever-opening-weekend-180-million-marvel-disney/.

33. Wikipedia, s.v. *Crazy Rich Asians* (film)," last edited June 25, 2023, https://en.wikipedia.org/wiki/Crazy_Rich_Asians_(film).

34. Mimi Aboubaker, "Data Obscures Positive Trends in VC Dollars Reaching Women-Founded Startups," TechCrunch, March 24, 2022, https://techcrunch.com/2022/03/24/data-obscures-positive-trends-in-vc-dollars-reaching-women-founded-startups/.

35. Gené Teare, "VC Funding to Black-Founded Startups Slows Dramatically as Venture Investors Pull Back," Crunchbase News, June 17, 2022, https://news.crunchbase.com/diversity/vc-funding-black-founded-startups/.